"In my 25 years in business, I have never met anyone to match Kevin's extraordinary appetite for action. He does for business what Nike does for sport."

Richard Hytner,
Deputy Chairman, Saatchi & Saatchi Worldwide

"A refreshingly different kind of business book, full of the straight-talking, no-nonsense and practical advice we have come to expect from Kevin Duncan. Also, lots of useful quotes throughout, and a very handy at-a-glance collection of summaries from the works of other business gurus"

Rita Clifton,
Non-Executive Director, Nationwide Building Society

"Kevin Duncan really nails the problem most of us face in dealing with the technology that is shaping our world."

Mark Earls,
author, *Herd*

"I currently have less than 20 emails in my inbox. Kevin, you made that happen."

Natalie Maher,
Communications Director, Design Business Association

"Kevin brings energy and passion to skills and personal development. He shows creativity and innovation in his approach to helping people get things done. His ideas and concepts take projects forward and add great momentum. His pragmatic approach and focus on results add clear direction – buy this book and learn."

Marie Petts,
Management Development Manager, News International

Tick Achieve

Tick Achieve

How to get stuff done

Kevin Duncan

Cartoons by Gray Jolliffe

CAPSTONE
be inspired!

John Wiley & Sons, Ltd

Other Wiley Editorial Offices

John Wiley & Sons Inc., 111 River Street, Hoboken, NJ 07030, USA

Jossey-Bass, 989 Market Street, San Francisco, CA 94103-1741, USA

Wiley-VCH Verlag GmbH, Boschstr. 12, D-69469 Weinheim, Germany

John Wiley & Sons Australia Ltd, 42 McDougall Street, Milton, Queensland 4064, Australia

John Wiley & Sons (Asia) Pte Ltd, 2 Clementi Loop #02-01, Jin Xing Distripark, Singapore 129809

John Wiley & Sons Canada Ltd, 22 Worcester Road, Etobicoke, Ontario, Canada M9W 1L1

Wiley also publishes its books in a variety of electronic formats. Some content that appears in
print may not be available in electronic books.

Library of Congress Cataloging-in-Publication Data

Duncan, Kevin, 1961-

    Tick achieve : how to get stuff done / Kevin Duncan ; cartoons by
Gray Jolliffe.

        p. cm.
    Includes index.

    ISBN 978-1-84112-795-8 (pbk. : alk. paper)

    1. Time management. 2. Achievement motivation. I. Jolliffe, Gray. II.
Title.

    HD69.T54.D86 2008

    650.1'1—dc22   2008001336

A catalogue record for this book is available from the British Library and the Library of Congress.
ISBN 13: 978-1-90646-527-8

Typeset by 11.5/14 ITC Garamond Light by Thomson Digital
Printed and Bound in Great Britain by T J International Ltd, Padtow, Cornwall, UK

Substantial discounts on bulk quantities of Capstone Books are available to corporations,
professional associations and other organizations. For details telephone John Wiley & Sons on
(+44)1243-770441, fax (+44) 1243 770571 or email corporatedevelopment@wiley.co.uk

To my mother Anne; my absolutely brilliant daughters Rosanna and Shaunagh; and Sarah Taylor, the Sleeping Lion.

In memory of my father James Grant Duncan, 1923–1989.

INTRODUCTION

This book is not designed to turn you into a machine for getting things done.

It is to help provide shape to what you do, so you can increase your chance of going home on time, not working the weekend, or not cancelling a holiday.

Too many people rush into doing large amounts of stuff when they haven't even thought about why they are doing them. Careful thought here removes the need for many tasks and improves clarity of thought.

Try some of the techniques and choose the ones that work best for you.

Learn how to celebrate little bits of progress, look down your list, tick off a job well done, and shout *Tick Achieve*.

Kevin Duncan,
Westminster, 2013

ABOUT THE AUTHOR

Kevin Duncan worked in advertising and direct marketing for twenty years. For the last thirteen years he has worked on his own as a business adviser, marketing expert and author. He advises various businesses as a non-executive director, business strategist and trainer.

He has two daughters, Rosanna and Shaunagh, and lives in Westminster. In his spare time he travels to strange parts of the world, releases rock albums and flies birds of prey.

Contact the author for advice and training:
kevinduncanexpertadvice@gmail.com
expertadviceonline.com
twitter: @kevinduncan

Also by the author:
Business Greatest Hits
How To Tame Technology
Marketing Greatest Hits
Marketing Greatest Hits Volume 2
Revolution
Run Your Own Business
Small Business Survival
So What?
Start
Start Your Own Business
The Diagrams Book
The Dictionary of Business Bullshit
What You Need To Know About Starting A Business

FOREWORD

In my 25 years in business, I have never met anyone to match Kevin's extraordinary appetite for action. He does for business what Nike does for sport.

I first learned how effective he was when I shared a desk with him in "The Nursery" at Benton & Bowles, where we both started as advertising graduate trainees. We were separated only by a desk-long divider. We could hear but not see each other. Each night at 18.00 (on the dot), I would hear Kevin on his side of the partition chanting, *"Tick Achieve, Tick Achieve, Tick Achieve"* as if in some kind of trance. It took a fortnight for rampant curiosity finally to overcome Nursery etiquette as I sneaked a swift look over the top. There I glimpsed Kevin, contentment oozing from every pore, "tick achieving", one by one, all the items on an immaculately laid out action list. I like him a lot now, but I hated him then. He's been "tick achieving" ever since.

Not too long ago, I asked Kevin to help me teach the Institute of Practitioners in Advertising's Excellence Diploma module on Brand Leadership. Who better to inspire a group of talented youngsters in the art of getting stuff done? As he sat down after his master class, I said to him that he really should pass on the Duncan strand of "Just Did It" DNA to as many people as possible. I suggested he should write a book about it. *"I'll put it on my list"*, he said. He did. And, true to form, he got it done. *Tick Achieve.*

Richard Hytner,
Deputy Chairman, Saatchi & Saatchi Worldwide

CONTENTS

Business Intelligence?

1

"The money is rolling in, but are we achieving anything?"

This chapter covers the "I'm too busy, I'm in a meeting" phenomenon. The difference between business and personal intelligence. What Tick Achieve does and does not mean. The power of the tick symbol. What achieve means and why achievement is not an endgame. Professional time wasting and why it happens. The need to see through the red mist of apparent busyness. Addiction to work and the modern curse of Work In Progress. How to think more and worry less, and how being organized lets you take it easy. Why outcome is more important than output, and why action is more important than activity. The first principles of cause and effect: "If I do x, then y will happen . . ." Why well-written lists matter and an outline of how to Tick Achieve.

"I'm too busy, I'm in a meeting."

Business intelligence?

It always used to be said that military intelligence was one of the best oxymorons around, along with deeply shallow and living death. But now it would appear that business intelligence is a new candidate. For every superbly run company that really knows what it is doing, there appear to be several more who cannot get even the simplest tasks done without a fiasco. Is this because they have inherently poor practices and systems, or is it simply because the people they employ cannot get things done in their own right? If it is the latter, then we may be facing a much more widespread problem – one in which millions of people are losing the art of getting things done.

There seems to be no shortage of personal intelligence, but still people struggle with completing all the things they intend to. The best-laid plans often remain just that: plans.

And yet there is little to beat that feeling when you've cleared your desk and there's nothing on your to-do list. It's brilliant. And I strongly believe that you can have a much better life if you get stuff done effectively. Once you get the hang of it, life gets so much easier, and you can really make yourself tick. Sleep better and worry less. Learn how to celebrate little bits of progress, look down your list, tick off a job well done, and shout *Tick Achieve*.

Tick Achieve: what does it mean?

Let me explain. To be able to tick a task off a list and move on to something else is at the very centre of human happiness. How so? Because humans are only happy when they do things. Sitting around just existing doesn't suit our make up. We have to feel that something is happening, and frequently it is much better that whatever it is has been self-generated. It's fine to enjoy the efforts of others, so long as you are contributing yourself, otherwise you would simply be the passive recipient of other people's ideas and actions.

Tick Achieve is my phrase for getting things done. It represents a thing well done, and a springboard for forward motion. It means you have delivered on your promise, whether to someone else, or to yourself. It means that you are the kind of person who always does what they say – a superb reputation to have. And it means that you never have to sit around saying *"I wish . . ."* or *"If only . . ."*

What does *Tick Achieve* not mean?

Let me be crystal clear at the outset what *Tick Achieve* does not mean. It does not mean the relentless pursuit of achievement at the expense of all else. It does not mean fighting your way to the top and pushing everybody else aside. It is not a mantra for irritating over-achievers who lack a generous view of the world. It is not a platform for bragging or gloating. It is simply a method by which individuals can get the small things done. Do enough of those, and the larger things start to fall into place too.

What is a tick?

Before we move on, let's just dissect the two words. Tick is a fascinating word, and has many meanings. Apart from parasites, alarm clock noises, twitching faces and colloquialisms such as giving someone a good ticking off, I want to highlight the two definitions that most help in the context of *Tick Achieve*.

Tick:
1. a moment or instant
2. a mark used to check off or indicate the correctness of something

---

Our life is full of moments. They all add up to days, months and years. Everything happens eventually, so long as you make it. And for those who make nothing happen, then what is the point of getting up in the morning? Fulfilment lies in the actual completion of things that contribute to your happiness and accumulate over time to a general feeling of well-being and achievement.

A physical tick, as in a near-V-shaped mark made with a pen to designate assent or completion, is a perfect distillation of a moment well spent. What a superb little symbol it is. It is positive. It means yes. It means go. It means job done. It means permission to move on. Just in two flicks of a pen. So my intention with *Tick Achieve* is to draw a straight line link between the symbol and the job done, so that you can derive maximum satisfaction from the progress that you make every day.

What does achieve mean?

To achieve comes from the old French word *achever*, to bring to an end. But over time it has gained some other subtleties that we will examine carefully in this book. Some modern interpretations of achievement have become sullied with the phenomenon of *over*-achievement, and much of the nastiness that can come with it.

Achieve:
1. bring to a successful conclusion
2. accomplish
3. attain
4. gain as by hard work or effort

Levels of achievement, and whether they are desirable or not, are hugely determined by the nature of the task, the number of them and the manner in which they are achieved. At bare minimum, the purpose of *Tick Achieve* is to equip you with the attitude and ability to complete simple, short tasks. The majority of these will be personal, and hugely to your advantage in leading a more fulfilled life. The same principles can also be applied, albeit in a stronger and more sustained form, to work ambitions and to complete more ambitious projects in life. That's about as far as *Tick Achieve* wants to go. This is not a manifesto for the relentless pursuit of status, the stockpiling of ludicrous amounts of cash, or the creation of a platform for transparent celebrity. We have enough over-rich people thumbing their noses at the rest of the world as it is.

Achievement is not an endgame

Who is to say if someone else is happy or not? We all know that a poor man can be significantly happier than a rich one. It's all relative. Simple jobs well done can generate far greater satisfaction than complicated ones that end messily, or that never end at all. If I am a recovering alcoholic, then to end the day without having had a drink is an achievement. If I am a soldier who has had his leg blown off and replaced with a prosthetic limb, then if I take my first step today, that's an achievement. If I am an overworked administrator and I complete a hundred tasks in a day, that's an achievement. You will know what represents an achievement to you, and each part of it might seem quite humble and insignificant. But if it matters to you, then it matters. There is no endgame. You don't have to end up a millionaire or ruling the country. We can all *Tick Achieve* and derive huge satisfaction from it.

Professional time wasting

It's an odd thing, but millions of people actually want to waste time. Think about it. You don't know how much time you have on this planet. You might get cancer or be killed in an accident tomorrow. So why would you want to hang about? Of course it depends to a degree on your level of ambition and ingenuity, but everybody wants to achieve something, even if it is to save enough for a holiday this year, be well regarded by their partner, or have a satisfied customer say thank you.

So why is it that so many people waste time? Some just can't see the point in getting on with it. They think it's all futile. Personally I think that's a shame and a lost opportunity. Every social study ever done shows that indolent people increase their happiness when they are given the chance (or a shove) to do something constructive. But in business, there is a much more cunning application of time wasting that is now quite commonplace. Many have spotted it, but few have said it out loud:

Most businesspeople want to waste time.

Before you send the lynch mob round to object to this apparently outrageous assertion, consider the following examples. They are all based on the universal law that the longer something takes, the more it costs.

1. Consultants

In their highly thought-provoking book *Dangerous Company*, James O'Shea and Charles Madigan highlight the extreme caution needed when dealing with management consultants. Over a series of rather shocking case histories, they tell of how consultants have been paid by the number of client staff they put out of work, how they have often replaced them in their own jobs and, crucially, how projects that were originally regarded as quick fixes have been dragged out for years. They warn against fuzzy concepts like "world class", which cannot be defined or measured, and creating a "consulting fantasyland", which sounds reassuring to companies but doesn't actually get them anywhere. There is a summary of the book in the Appendix.

Just before he died, James McKinsey, founder of today's massive consulting firm, poignantly confessed that making real decisions in business is actually a lot harder than getting paid to advise people what to do – sometimes it is fine to admit that you don't have all the answers. Better that than hanging around only to discover that you don't.

2. Lawyers and accountants

If it's complicated, it will take a long time, won't it? That's why many technical professions surround themselves with impenetrable jargon. Lawyers and accountants are two particularly guilty parties. If you can't understand what they are talking about, then you have to have their services. It's a deliberate policy called obfuscation.

Obfuscation: The act or an instance of making something deliberately obscure or difficult to understand.

The papers are full of examples every week of legal and monetary cases that have dragged on for years. Each side is trying to run rings round the other and wrap them up in red tape and complication. The longer it goes on, the more they get paid.

3. Builders

Builders are a classic example of a trade where time equals money. The cost of the materials can be ascertained approximately even by the purchaser, so the only flexible variable is the time taken to complete the job. And of course, you can't abandon the job before it's finished because your home won't have a roof, or whatever vital element is left missing.

I could go on. There are many specific businesses where it pays to waste time. The practice is also rife in general commerce. If you really want to *Tick Achieve*, you need to see this strange smokescreen for what it is, and work out whether you have become caught up in it yourself. I call it red mist.

Seeing through the red mist

Stage one in getting more done yourself is to realize that many people don't want to get things done. It sounds strange but it's true. As well as the professions above, there are millions of people in general commerce whose main objective is to do as little as possible. It's human nature. You only have to analyse the number of sick days after Bank Holidays and weekends to prove the point statistically.

> *"They intoxicate themselves with work so they won't see how they really are."*
>
> **Aldous Huxley, quoted in The E-Myth**

But there is a much more insidious angle to non-doers in business. These are the people who are in the office all the time, looking as though they are frantically busy, when in fact they are achieving little or nothing. This is what the Italians call the "English Disease". A lot appears to be happening because everyone is rushing around, but nothing really is. That's the red mist. The tragedy of this is that a huge number of people who do this do not even realize that they are doing it.

Addicted to work

Workaholism is now a recognized phenomenon. In New York, they have Workaholics Anonymous groups whose aim is to help people who work compulsively. In a supreme twist of irony, many members are apparently too busy to attend. A 2007 survey by the Center for Work – Life Policy, a New York-based non-profit group, revealed that 45% of executives were "extreme" workers (*Sunday Times*, 10 June 2007). And yet there is no correlation between all this extra "work" and any increase in productivity in companies. The advent of technology that keeps people in touch every hour of the day creates the impression of busyness, but doesn't actually contribute to anything. The best one can say about it is that there can be a link between high levels of work activity and high self-esteem. But in truth, this is all part of the red mist too. Pejorative words such as workaholism simply get replaced with driven, energetic or ambitious in an attempt to make them sound beneficial.

The modern curse of WIP

All of which amounts to a lot of rushing around, but is anything actually getting done? And if so, are they the right things? In many instances, there are undoubtedly too many balls in the air at once. As a colleague of mine once observed: *"There are fifteen balls in the air on this project, and two of them are mine."*

WIP is the contemporary acronym for Work In Progress. And what a disaster it is. So pervasive has this phenomenon become that it is almost a discipline in its own right. To highlight the futility of WIP, consider this. A task is only of value if it is finished. The longer it isn't, the worse things are. Many modern businesspeople would do well to remember that. As Fergus O'Connell states in his excellent book *Simply Brilliant*: "Things either are or they aren't." There is a summary in the Appendix. Hiding mountains of unfinished work under the broad banner of WIP is hopeless.

> *"The middle of every project looks like a disaster."*
>
> **Rosabeth Moss**

Yes, but have you actually done it?

Dreamers, and those who are incapable of completing any-thing, spend their whole life saying *"I've got a great idea!"* whilst simultaneously being ridiculed by their colleagues and friends as being pathologically incapable of getting anything done. The indolent husband whose wife points out that he still hasn't put the shelves up after three years is more than just an invention of comedians. It's a very com-mon problem.

How to think more and worry less

It's about time we started valuing mental activity as much as, or more than, physical activity. A carefully applied thought can achieve far more than an infinite number of meetings. Individuals need to realize this, and companies really should have worked it out years ago. Fretting about issues and generating a big head of steam has no beneficial effect on the outcome. In fact, the opposite may well be true. The knack lies in a calm assessment of the situation, and a judi-cious application of the right remedy. This may only take a few minutes. And if it did, what on earth would all those supposedly busy executives do for the rest of the week?

How being organized lets you take it easy

This is where a massive distinction becomes evident between those who want to get things done and those who don't. In the main, individuals want to get things done in their personal lives. So do self-employed people, because if they don't, they don't get paid, and in some cases there is no one else to do it anyway. The ones who don't want to get things done usually work for companies. That's because they are going to get paid the same amount regardless of what they do. But they can't let it appear as though nothing is happening, so they generate activities to cover it up. It's that red mist again.

What sorted individuals and self-employed people have worked out is that the more organized they are, the easier they can do their work. That means less stress, quicker delivery and, fantastically, more free time. This is the polar opposite of the corporate executive who, if they finish their work too efficiently, simply get given more. That's why they spin it out. So if you are a company person, you will have to try extra hard to shed your work habits and make some changes in your personal life. We will look at all this in the coming chapters.

Outcome not output

So, assuming you do want to get things done (otherwise why would you have read this far?), we need to get to grips with some of the things that prevent people from doing just that.

> *"I am rather like a mosquito in a nudist camp. I know what I want to do, but I don't know where to begin."*
>
> **Stephen Bayne, quoted in Getting Things Done**

Making a start is half the battle, and we will look at this in some detail. If there is a lot confronting you, it can be hard to know where to start. The amount of output you generate is irrelevant. When it comes to getting things done, we are interested solely in the outcome. That may well mean only doing the bits that can directly affect the outcome, not all the other static that seems related but isn't central.

Action not activity

Confusing action and activity is a common thing. Much activity is essentially pointless. It may appear to contribute to the main objective, but in fact it doesn't. In truth, lots of people intentionally fool themselves in this respect. They want to believe that things are complicated to justify the fact that they haven't yet done them, or that it is taking a long time to do. Displacement activities are common too. So much of what is going on is either intentionally disguised to look as though it matters, or even worse, the doer of the activity genuinely believes it will help when in fact it won't. We will work hard to try to disentangle this problem.

> *"Every morning in Africa, a gazelle wakes up. It knows it must run faster than the fastest lion or it will be killed. Every morning a lion wakes up. It knows it must outrun the slowest gazelle or it will starve to death. It doesn't matter whether you are a lion or a gazelle, when the sun comes up, you'd better be running."*
>
> **African proverb, quoted on Radio 4**

Cause and effect: first principles

At the heart of solving the inertia problem is the ability to determine genuine cause and effect. It's a hell of a skill and many people simply don't have it. It is essential to master the basic art of working out what will happen if you do something, or to put it simply:

"If I do x, then y will happen . . ."

This works on three crucial dimensions:

1. If I do x, then y will happen: I want y to happen.
2. If I do x, then y will happen: I do not want y to happen.

If you are a mature *Tick Achiever*, then you will have worked out the direct link between x and y, and more often than not you will elicit the response in example number one. You do something and expect something to happen. That's why you did it.

If you don't think much about your actions, then you will often experience the state of affairs in example two. You do plenty of things, but they don't lead to the action or reaction that you want or expect.

But much more crucially in the context of *Tick Achieve* is the third possibility:

3. If I do x, then y will happen: y is irrelevant to what I want done.

Herein lies the crux of most people's problems when it comes to getting things done. They work pretty hard. They initiate lots of things. They even finish lots of things. And those things have no bearing whatsoever on the main point.

Most of what people do has nothing to do with the main point.

What's on *your* list?

That's what this book is all about: working out what matters and what doesn't. This will enable you to do less and get more done. As well as mastering the basics of cause and effect, we will look at the dreaded subject of lists. These are usually at the core of anyone's activity, and they have a lot to answer for. Call them what you want: to-do lists, checklists, action lists. They all amount to the same thing – a prompt for you to get things done. And if the list is confusing or unhelpful, then the resulting action will be too.

How many times have you thought of something crucial to do and then forgotten it completely? That's why people invented lists. And very useful they can be too. If, and only if, they are written properly and used effectively. Put thirty things on a list, and it becomes too daunting. Put three things on it, and there's no point in having a list at all.

In truth, most lists are randomly assembled. They do little to help you get things done. After all, that's the only point of a list. We will look at the art of great list writing in detail in Chapter 5. As a trainee I used to annoy all my colleagues by ticking everything off before I went to the pub. It's not a competitive thing – it's so you can enjoy your free time safe in the knowledge that you've got things under control.

How to *Tick Achieve*

So, to recap on the main points of this introductory chapter:

• There is no point in appearing to be busy, when you aren't actually getting anything done.

- Much so-called business intelligence isn't that intelligent.
- It will help you to "unlearn" many business practices to liberate more of your personal intelligence.
- A tick is a great symbol of getting something done.
- Small achievements are more important than the pursuit of something grandiose.
- As such, achievement in the lofty sense of the word is not an endgame in itself.
- Many businesspeople actually want to waste time, either because they want to charge more or because it fills their time and they get paid the same anyway.
- You need to see your way through this red mist to something clearer.
- Many people are addicted to work as an end in itself – don't let that be you.
- Work in progress is a misleading smokescreen for a job not done.
- Perpetual dreamers never get round to doing anything – don't let that be you.
- The more you think, the less you will have to do.
- The more organized you are, the more you can take it easy.
- Outcome is more important that output.
- Action is more important than activity.
- Most of what people do has nothing to do with the main point.
- It is crucial that you understand cause and effect when it comes to your actions.
- "If I do x, then y will happen . . ." holds the key to almost everything.
- The manner in which you construct your lists will have a fundamental bearing on your ability to get things done.

What's to come?

The book contains lots of techniques tried and tested on scores of individuals over the last 30 years. To give you a taster, they include:

- **Talk straight.** The more you waffle, the less clear you are about what you really need to do. This is the theme of the next chapter.
- **Leave it out.** The more you exclude, the easier it is to get the important things done. We look at this in Chapter 3, which explains how to write an anti list. That's a list of what you are *not* going to do.
- **One in a row.** Little things can make a massive difference, and you only need small steps to make progress. Don't let the so-called big picture paralyse what you are trying to do. We celebrate this in Chapter 4.
- **Tick Achieve.** By Chapter 5 we are ready to work out how to turn this into a way of life. We also examine the art of great list writing.
- **Look lively.** None of this works unless you apply the right levels of energy and application to the task in hand. Don't be fooled though – we are more interested in mental than physical energy. Chapter 6 explains how it works.
- **Outthink yourself.** With some judicious self-realization, you can counteract your failings. It's not difficult. Chapter 7 outlines tripwires and fail-safes that make sure you never forget anything.
- **Progress not perfection.** Many people never get things done because they are striving for perfection, which never arrives. Chapter 8 establishes the distinction between once-in-a-lifetime nirvana and the millions of other things that just need to get done.

- *Making business tick.* Chapter 9 attempts to draw all this together and suggest how it can usefully be applied in a business context.
- *Make yourself tick.* And finally we round off with all the personal applications of how you can *Tick Achieve* and a summary of the overall method.

Thinking and
Talking
Straight

"Look at it this way—Shakespeare
did what it would take a million
monkeys eternity to do".

This chapter covers how people who are incapable of coming to the point are literally pointless. The new world of waffle and different types, including strategic and internal waffle. How you can't think straight if you can't talk straight. Duckspeak and Birtspeak. How a strategy is simply when you have decided what to do. The rise of Offlish. Mission Incomprehensible and the fine art of business fiction. Understanding how language works. Pleonasms and circumlocution. Permission to talk straight: if you must use jargon at work, do not use it at home. The mate, mum or grandmother test, and an outline of how to talk straight.

People who are incapable of coming to the point are literally pointless.

The new world of waffle

It used to be so simple. You only have to watch an old black and white film to see that. In the "olden days" people used to talk straight. They would choose their words carefully, and quite right too, because words are powerful things. I'm not entirely sure when the change started, but I can certainly remember clear language being the norm throughout the seventies. There was some nonsense when I took my first trainee job in 1982, but nothing on the scale of today. It was probably the nineties when it really started taking over, and now it seems to be the norm.

Waffle, spin, bullshit, call it what you like. It's the enemy of clear thought. And if you can't think clearly, then you can't act clearly. Too many companies and individuals have lost the capacity to express themselves clearly, and I am convinced this retards their ability to get things done effectively. It follows logically that if you can't come to the point verbally then you will have extreme difficulty doing it physically. Coming to the point in words helps you to take action in reality. The corollary of this is that if you are incapable of coming to the point, then you will not have one, and so be pointless. I don't mean this in the broad sense of being a pointless person, I simply mean that at that particular moment, on that particular subject matter, you will have no clarity of thought or deed.

> *"Reality is just a crutch for people who can't deal with drugs."*
>
> **Robin Williams, quoted in**
> **The Sunday Telegraph**

You can't talk straight if you can't think straight.

Talking straight is a vital component of getting things done. This has multiple applications. Look at some of these possibilities:

State of affairs	Likely outcome
Boss waffles	Subordinates cannot take suitable action
Staff waffle	Boss is misinformed and cannot take appropriate action
Friend waffles	Other friends cannot react specifically
Partner waffles	Other partner misses the point
Parent waffles	Child is confused
Child waffles	Parent is none the wiser

Of course, not every exchange of words requires action. Even if none is required, the residual effect of waffle will be confusion, boredom, lack of respect and absence of clarity. But if action is required, then it is essential that the communicator does a good job of explaining what the proposed action is. Having the words spoken out loud at least gives the listeners the opportunity to establish that they have been subjected to waffling. This enables them to compare notes, take the mickey, ask for clarification, or simply ignore the request on the grounds that it is unintelligible. There is, however, something much more dangerous than this when it comes to getting things done.

The curse of internal waffle

My definition of internal waffle is talking rubbish to yourself. It sounds near impossible, but millions of people do it. You can just hear the words, unspoken, rattling around in their heads as they embark on a marathon bout of self-delusion. Spoken waffle has a deep bearing on this, because it promotes an environment in which nonsense is regarded as normal. It's insidious stuff, and arguably even more potent when unsaid than when uttered out loud.

Internal wafflers believe their own propaganda and base decisions on it, often important ones. They then regurgitate their muddled thinking as requests to others, often causing chaos in the process. This is fuzzy thinking, and is the arch-enemy of everything that *Tick Achieve* stands for. (This should not be confused with fuzzy logic, that venerable branch of logic that allows computers to deal with imprecise data.)

Duckspeak and Birtspeak

In his book *1984*, George Orwell introduced the idea of duckspeak to describe the stale, ritualistic official language of the Big Brother state. This language was deliberately emptied of meaning, and used to show the loyalty of the speaker or writer to the ruling ideology. A succinct description of it is contained in Richard Heller's excellent book *High Impact Speeches*:

> *"George Orwell would be despondent but not surprised by the state of the English language today. In 1984, he predicted the phenomenon of 'duckspeak', words intended to mean nothing and designed to show mindless acceptance of the values and mentality of its originators. Orwell's 'duckspeak' was originated by the ruling party in a totalitarian dictatorship. It was part of the general phenomenon of Newspeak, language so shrivelled in meaning that it would not allow people to think differently from the ruling party.*
>
> *Although we do not have a one-party state, we hear even more duckspeak than Orwell predicted. It is created not only by governments but by various professions and special interest groups, and for the same reason as Orwell's in 1984. Duckspeak serves to identify people who are totally loyal to the values of the originating group, and it deprives them of the chance to think any other way."*

There is a summary of Richard's book in the Appendix. As he rightly points out, today duckspeak is very much the norm. This sort of stuff can come from professions such as economics, management consultancy, sociology, marketing and psychology, but the biggest culprit is undoubtedly modern government. Almost unbelievably, its purpose is not so much to communicate as to identify where the speaker belongs. So if you work in a company, take care to distinguish this background of vague static from clear, actionable words and ideas. If you listen to the news a lot, then make sure that you retain the power to work out the difference between meaningless collections of words and precise pronouncements. And if you work for yourself, don't start speaking that way yourself. An ability to speak clearly will be essential when you try to think clearly, and translate those thoughts into sensible action.

Orwell's vision was fictional, albeit highly accurate in its prediction. But much of this talk happens every day in companies across the world, and it has been highly ridiculed in certain places. "Birtspeak" was a phrase coined by the satirical magazine *Private Eye* to describe the use of the impenetrable jargon used by Sir John Birt, then the Director-General of the BBC. Here's an example:

> *"We need to establish a less prescriptive corporate framework which offers business units greater flexibility within the parameters of common core corporate guidelines."*

You could fill a book with this stuff and be none the wiser. Ironically, Birt came to the BBC when it had a worldwide reputation for the good use of English, and left it with a worldwide reputation for managerial cant.

Successful *Tick Achievers* must resist the temptation to speak like this at all costs.

There's waffle, and there's strategic waffle

Some waffle is easy to spot. As such, it causes a lot less trouble than disguised waffle – that is to say, waffle that sounds as though it is legitimate language serving a useful purpose. The cleverest (or stupidest) way to disguise waffle is to file it under the broad banner of "strategy". The devilish part of this is that the waffler has the perfect get-out clause: if you, the listener, don't understand it, then you must be dim because you don't "get the strategy". This is upside down thinking. Let's just consider for a moment what a strategy is:

Strategy:
1. the art of the planning of a war
2. a particular long-term plan for success
3. a plan or stratagem

The first definition tallies perfectly with much of modern business language. It's all so macho, isn't it? Campaigns, targets and missions. There are even those who forge a direct link between warfare and business. *Sun Tzu: The Art Of War For Executives*, by Donald Krause, is a classic example. Don't get me wrong: judicious learning from other disciplines can be beneficial, and in fact I have read and summarized the book for you in the Appendix. However, if taken the wrong way, the whole process of comparing war with business can lead to overly macho approaches. To be fair, this is not really what the book is all about, but it is obsessed with the competition ("the enemy"), whereas I would argue that it is more profitable to concentrate on what *you* are going to do, not the opposition. All the top sports managers say it: concentrate on what you are going to do – don't worry about the other lot.

The second definition of strategy, a particular long-term plan for success, is spot on. Crucially though, what it doesn't say is "a particular long-term plan for success wrapped up in impenetrable language that confuses everybody". Once again, the simpler the message, the more likely it is to get done.

The third definition, a plan or stratagem, is a touch more sinister. A stratagem is a plan or trick to deceive an enemy, and really should have nothing to do with strategy at all. Once you strip away all the waffle, it is actually quite simple to define what a strategy is:

A strategy is simply when you have decided what to do.

It's your plan, and as such a great basis for getting things done. So by all means call your plan for getting things done a strategy, but don't let the language slip into waffle. It is also crucial not to confuse strategy with tactics. Strategy is long-term – tactics are short-term. Strategy is broad – tactics are detailed. They are not the same thing. One strategy may include many tactics.

The rise of Offlish

It's not as easy as you might think to spot waffle. Many words can have precious little meaning when you strip them down, and meaning is what we are looking for. Because without meaning, you won't know what you are doing, or what to do next. Carl Newbrook, in his book *The A–Z of Offlish*, attempts to make sense of workplace jargon. *Offlish* is an elision of Office and English. It is nigh on impossible to summarize such a book, but here is a flavour of the sort of stuff that he is trying to decipher.

Ask, big: a difficult task. Every day in the office there's a mountain to climb.
Bandwidth: the capacity of a communication channel. Always too small to be effective.
Ducks in a row: preparedness; show of unity. A delightful, if rare, sight.
Eleventh hour, at the: a late intervention. The point at which a senior manager becomes involved in a piece of work.

Face time: a meeting. A formal rendezvous. The ability to converse is one of the things that distinguishes man from the animals.
Gas, cooking with: achieving peak performance.
Interface: a boundary; to interact.
Knitting, stick to the: to avoid complication.
Legs: longevity.
Mile, go the extra: strenuous and special exertion.
Park it: set aside an issue or question.
Pear-shaped, go: awry.
Ramp up: to increase or improve effort.
Sub-optimal: less than a total success.
Upscale: to increase resources.
Value-added: something additional to a product or service that makes it more valuable to the customer.
Wash its face: break even.

Many of you will recognize this sort of stuff all too well. It's also easy to deride, but I am sure we have all slipped into this sort of language at some point. I include myself in that observation and, believe me, I struggle every day to avoid it, whilst still often failing. Being thoroughly on the alert for cliché and jargon is a good quality to develop if you want to *Tick Achieve*. You'll find a fairly comprehensive list of offenders in one of my previous books, So What? (chapter 4).

Mission Incomprehensible

Whilst individuals can be guilty of spouting incomprehensible words, companies are just as bad, and nowhere can we observe better examples of corporate double-speak than in their mission statements. In the egregious examples below, I have simply replaced the company name or the sector they work in with an x. See if you can make any sense of them.

"As pioneers of x, it is time for us to trail-blaze again. We passionately believe x has a future, but only if we stop interrupting what people are interested in. Time is the new currency, and the audience is the new client. We are going to be pioneers in the land beyond the moment."

"At x world group, our mission is to be recognised as a Category of One in our ability to create x for our clients, brands and services. To do so, we know we must bring together the right mix of capabilities invisibly in order to deliver visibly powerful results in the market place. We have the power and the passion to achieve this vision, because we have: a leading global x; world-class companies in seven disciplines and top-tier talent in each; a full range of capabilities – more than most holding companies; a winning culture – people who love the business, who don't give up or give in; key clients who understand the vital role of x and want our help. Our strategy for achieving this vision is built on our commitment to a core principle: 'To be the best in each market and in every discipline in which we operate.'"

"We think it is better to outsmart the competition than outspend them. We think x should be part of an idea rather than ideas part of an x. We think ideas are only big enough if they work wherever they land. And we think the answer is more important than how you get there."

"Fuel. Nothing in this world happens without it. From cars to rockets to the human body, fuel powers everything. It is the energy that begets vitality and triggers forward motion. X needs fuel for the very same reasons. To power advancement. Stimulate growth. And to provide the momentum behind a well-planned journey. At x, we are the fuel that powers that growth."

"At the heart of x there is La Difference . . . each specific approach builds our strength as a Groupe. Across each brand and entity, each team, we dedicate all our energy to the success of our clients . . . the values that lead us are: pioneer and challenger; multi-cultural and creative; innovative and agile; humanist and accountable."

"You might expect a mission statement at this point. We don't have one. Instead, we have a Purpose, with four components. Our Inspirational Dream: to be revered as the hothouse of world-changing x that transforms our clients' businesses. Our Greatest Imaginable Challenge: to win our revenue and profit race by selling the most highly valued x. Our Focus: to create and perpetuate x. Our Spirit: one team, one dream. Nothing is impossible."

"X is a highly competitive industry. X is a leading global x, providing world-class x management services. We create x that produce results. Our services cover the full spectrum of x needs – channel strategy, planning, consulting, post-campaign analysis, financial control and ROI. Our success is based on looking beyond the ordinary into the extraordinary. Strong strategic understanding underlies everything we do, and our business is built on the foundation of relationships. We aim to exceed your expectations. We ask more questions, take the initiative. We expect more. Our clients can always expect more."

"We believe in x. In their power. In their value. Their increasingly important place in consumers' lives. More than just a goodwill entry on a corporate balance sheet, an x is the single most important asset any company has. We believe our job is to help clients build enduring x that live as a part of consumers' lives and command their loyalty and confidence. How we go about doing this is through a proprietary way of thinking and working that we call 360 Degree X Stewardship. We believe our role as 360 degree stewards is this: creating attention-getting messages that make a

promise consistent and true to the x and guiding actions, both big and small, that deliver on that promise. To every audience that x has. At every intersection point. At all times."

"In a world where the Prosumer shapes the marketplace, marketers need more than good x. Marketers need x to drive profitable growth. X that transforms the product, the brand, the company, and what allows us to deliver x is the Power of One."

I trust that is all crystal clear. Frankly, I have nothing to add.

The fine art of business fiction

In the same way that most history is written in a thoroughly biased way by the victors, the business world is rife with case histories of apparently astonishing success in the face of stiff competition. But many of these are essentially fiction. Take any successful company, and you will find scores of related case studies that claim variously that it was all down to the management, one particular leader, the supply chain, product quality, staff motivation schemes, or customer loyalty initiatives. All you have to do, apparently, is copy their approach in order to emulate their success. This is patently disingenuous nonsense, otherwise everybody would be doing it.

In his book *The Halo Effect*, subtitled . . . *and the Eight Other Business Delusions That Deceive Managers*, Phil Rosenzweig cites numerous examples of flawed logic, confused thinking and unscientific evidence that are used by business gurus. Most of the secrets of success and the measures they use to "prove" them are nothing of the sort, he suggests. One reason for this is the halo effect (something psychologists have long understood), where if a person or company seems successful in a way that we admire, everything they do seems worth emulating. Take a simple example. It has been "proved" many times over that happy staff means happy customers and shareholders. But the so-called proof is based on staff morale comparisons between successful and unsuccessful companies. In which case, the cause and effect may work in precisely the opposite direction, so that failure makes people miserable and success makes people happy. It's perfectly possible.

The question is: are these delusions maliciously intentional? If so, then they come under the heading of lying. In his thought-provoking book *Liar's Paradise*, Graham Edmonds says that 80% of companies think that they are fraud-free, but a recent survey actually revealed fraud in 45% of them. He outlines seven degrees of deceit:

1. **White lie:** told to make someone feel better or to avoid embarrassment.
2. **Fib:** relatively insignificant, such as excuses and exaggerations.
3. **Blatant:** whoppers used when covering up mistakes or apportioning blame.
4. **Bullshit:** a mixture of those above combined with spin and bluff to give the best impression.
5. **Political:** similar to bullshit but with much bigger scale and profile.
6. **Criminal:** illegal acts from fraud to murder, and their subsequent denial.
7. **Ultimate:** so large that it must be true. As Joseph Goebbels said: *"If you tell a lie big enough and keep repeating it, people will eventually come to believe it."*

Both books are summarized in the Appendix.

Spotting waffle

So we have asserted beyond doubt that we live in a tricky verbal world. What can you do about it? Here is the *Tick Achieve* ten-point guide to spotting deceptive waffle. Remember: a lot of the language is very hard to penetrate, so you need to listen hard and question very deeply. Check any statement or request for action for the following:

1. False arguments
If you know your facts and the other person is incorrect, then you shouldn't act on their instructions. In fact, you may not even be able to.

2. Circular arguments
If the person in question keeps returning to the same point, then there may only be one point. If it's valid, then fine. If it's not, do not act on it.

3. Repetition
Similar to the circular argument, but not quite the same. In the circular example, the speaker will head off elsewhere and then return. In the case of repetition, they just keep saying the same thing, albeit using different words.

4. Incorrect conclusions
These are what I call "synapse jumps" and what the Romans called a non sequitur. The synapse is the point at which a nerve impulse is relayed from the terminal portion of an axon to the dendrites of an adjacent neuron. The charge jumps the gap to let your brain know what's going on. Many speakers jump a gap and end up in completely the wrong place. A non sequitur is just that: a statement that has little or no relevance to what preceded it – literally: *"it does not follow"*.

5. Spurious sources

Some people make themselves sound authentic by quoting sources, but they may not be valid. Check these assertions carefully and question them closely.

6. Irrelevance

It is extraordinary the amount of irrelevant material that is wheeled out to validate a point. In fact, the more evidence is offered, the more inquisitive you might wish to be – the *"Thou doth protest too much"* syndrome.

7. Weak points

Most decent cases either argue for themselves or have one or two solid support points. If someone puts up a chart with support points, the weak points at the end always undermine the strong points at the beginning. If this is the case, review the entire argument.

8. Cliché and jargon

Don't trust it. It is usually disguising something.

9. Inconsistency

Inconsistency is to be viewed suspiciously if it appears in the same speech or written piece. But also keep an eye out for it over time. Many people gainsay themselves in subsequent statements.

10. Vagueness

Vagueness should be easy to spot. If the person can't come to the point, or clearly hasn't got one, then don't do what they say.

Understand how language works

The great thing about concentrating on how language works is that you gain two fundamental benefits:

1. You can identify when someone else is not talking straight.
2. You can talk straight yourself.

In that respect, if you are looking for guidance on how to talk straight, then all you need to be able to do is identify all the things we have looked at in this chapter, and avoid them. At bare minimum, by avoiding false and circular arguments, repetition, incorrect conclusions, spurious sources, irrelevance, weak points, cliché and jargon, inconsistency and vagueness you will automatically be talking straight. There is more you can do, however.

Try to understand the correct definitions of figures of speech and use them appropriately. When used in the right context, they can enhance communication and understanding. We have said enough about their incorrect use. Here's a quick guide to their correct use, drawing in large part from Richard Heller's *High Impact Speeches*.

Analogy: a comparison made to show a similarity. What in the everyday world gives an accurate representation of the obscure thing I want to describe?

The texture of his skin was like orange peel.

Hyperbole: deliberate exaggeration for effect.

He embraced her a thousand times.

Metaphor: a word or phrase applied to something to which it does not literally apply.

He was a lion in battle.

Oxymoron: putting two apparently contradictory words together.

> *Deeply shallow. Military intelligence. Exquisite torture.*

Paradox: something which appears illogical but in fact makes sense.

> *I don't want to belong to any club that would have me as a member* (Groucho Marx).

Simile: a figure of speech that likens one thing to another from a different category, preceded by *as* or *like.*

> *His speech was like a wet sponge.*

All of these approaches have their place, if used correctly. There are some, however, that rarely help.

Pleonasms and circumlocution

Pleonasms and circumlocution are the two great enemies of clear speech. A pleonasm is where somebody deliberately uses extra words that add nothing. For example:

- *Well I have never seen anything like that in all of my born days.* (I have never seen that before)
- *In this day and age.* (Today)
- *At this moment in time.* (Now)
- *In the final analysis.* (Ultimately)
- *The position in regard to cats.* (Cats)

Circumlocution is an indirect way of expressing something, such as:

Consideration of accessibility issues in relation to transport nodes is of paramount importance. (We must think about transport)

Neither of these approaches helps your ability to talk straight. Also avoid:

1. Pointless modifiers.

   Quite important
   Relatively insignificant

2. Pointless phrases beginning with "it".

   It should be remembered that . . .

3. Sentences that simply repeat what has already been said. One of these sentences can go:

   The report could not attempt to be comprehensive. It deals with some issues more thoroughly than others.

Permission to talk straight

Strangely, some people feel that they do not have permission to talk straight, but it is essential that we do. Even if you work in a corporate culture that promotes the sort of expression we have looked at in this chapter, you still have two choices:

1. Deliberately talk straight at work and stand out as a result.
2. Talk like them at work but talk straight at home.

Ideally, one would hope that you choose to do both. That way, there will be a close fit between your on- and off-duty persona, and you will be a well-rounded character. If you feel you need to go for option two, then fair enough, but be aware of something very important:

If you must use jargon at work, do not use it at home.

> *"The difficult we do immediately. The impossible takes a little longer."*
>
> **US Army Corps motto**

The longer you work for a company, the harder that may become. Cutting through it and moving on to clearer things is essential to your ability to *Tick Achieve*. There is a straight line link between talking straight and getting things done, so at the very least you need to have a clear head and level expression at home in order to sort out your personal life. Never tell your partner or children that you will *"deal with it offline"*.

The mate, mum or grandmother test

The best way to determine whether you are talking straight is to try it out on your mum, your grandmother or a mate in the pub. Even if they can't be there in person, imagine whether they would know what you were talking about. Would they understand it? If no, then change it. Does it sound daft? If so, then change it. Do you feel stupid when you hear the words out loud? If yes, then change it.

> *"You do not really understand something until you can explain it to your grandmother."*
>
> **Albert Einstein**

How to think and talk straight

To summarize the main points in this chapter:

- People who are incapable of coming to the point are literally pointless.
- Do not talk like this, otherwise you will be unclear about what to do, and this will prevent you from being able to *Tick Achieve.*
- This can have very bad consequences, the worst of which is that you can't talk straight if you can't think straight.
- The new world of waffle is beguiling and deceptive – if you can, play no part in it.
- The curse of internal waffle refers to those who are incapable of being honest with themselves – this is the archenemy of getting things done effectively.
- There's waffle and there's strategic waffle – strategic waffle is additionally dangerous because it sounds as though it means something when in fact it often doesn't.
- A strategy is simply when you have decided what to do – keep your expression straightforward.
- Spotting waffle is an important trait to develop – it prevents you from being fooled on the one hand, and shows you what phraseology to avoid on the other.
- Understanding how language works has a huge bearing on your ability to speak and think clearly – learn as much as you can.
- Pleonasms and circumlocution are to be avoided whenever possible.
- You have permission to talk straight, and should do it at work and home if possible.
- If you must use jargon at work, do not use it at home.
- Use the mate, mum or grandmother test to find out whether you are talking (and therefore probably thinking) nonsense.

Leave it Out

3

"I hope to god it's urgent."

This chapter covers how brevity equals intelligence and less really is more. The Laws of Simplicity *and how eliminating issues produces faster answers. The power of asking: does this need to be done at all? Extraneous extraction and how leaving it out forces the issue. Reductionism: think harder and simplify everything. Boxy minds and why they help. The value of anti lists. Why tasks do not improve in quality if they are delayed. How to do less and get more done. Towards a manifesto for* Tick Achieve*: say no more often, debate hard and early, have a system. Once you have written a task down you can forget about it. Trust your* Depth Mind*, kick bad habits and pose Killer Questions. Outline of how to leave it out.*

Brevity equals intelligence.

Less really is more

So now we get down to the tough action required to ensure that you can actually get done the things that matter to you. We have looked in some detail at the prevailing mood of much modern speech – long-winded, circuitous and not necessarily very well thought out. The assumption at this stage is that you have the desire and the wherewithal to talk straight – that is to say, you can construct clear, jargon-free sentences and say them out loud. This is not to sound patronizing – there are many that can't. The clarity of your spoken approach will have a direct bearing on your ability to convert them into rapid, effective action.

Now we turn our attention to the small matter of brevity. Brevity equates to intelligence. The less time it takes to articulate a point, the better expressed it is. Hence the title of this chapter: *Leave it out.* The more you leave out, the closer you get to the heart of the matter. Blaise Pascal, the scientist and philosopher who lived in the 1600s, had the right idea:

> *"I have made this longer than usual because I have not had the time to make it shorter."*
>
> **Blaise Pascal**

The first draft of any presentation, speech or thinkpiece may well include all sorts of broad material, but it is not until careful thought is applied to the central line of argument that much of it can be discarded. More material does not necessarily strengthen an argument. In some complex academic and technical areas it might, but in most areas of life, and certainly the business of getting things done, it doesn't. Skilful editing and the ability to filter out extraneous material is a crucial asset for anyone who wants to *Tick Achieve* effectively. We will use the principle of extraneous extraction in a moment.

You will probably have heard the expression that less is more. This is the notion that simplicity and clarity lead to good design. It is a 19th-century proverbial phrase, of unknown origin, but often associated with the architect and furniture designer Ludwig Mies Van Der Rohe (1886–1969), one of the founders of modern architecture and a proponent of simplicity of style. He was also the man behind *"God is in the details"*. With regard to *Tick Achieve*, less definitely is more, by which I mean that the less you concentrate on, the more you will get done in total. To be able to reduce your list of tasks to something smaller or more manageable, you need some rules and approaches.

The Laws of Simplicity

The Laws of Simplicity is a thought-provoking book by John Maeda, who is a graphic designer, visual artist and computer scientist at the Massachusetts Institute of

Technology. He has even gone so far as to set up the SIMPLICITY Consortium at the MIT Media Lab, so he clearly believes in it.

He asserts quite simply that simplicity = sanity, and goes on to outline ten laws of simplicity:

1. *Reduce.* The simplest way to achieve simplicity is through thoughtful reduction.
2. *Organize.* Organization makes a system of many appear fewer.
3. *Time.* Savings in time feel like simplicity.
4. *Learn.* Knowledge makes everything simpler.
5. *Differences.* Simplicity and complexity need each other.
6. *Context.* What lies in the periphery of simplicity is definitely not peripheral.
7. *Emotion.* More emotions are better than less.
8. *Trust.* In simplicity we trust.
9. *Failure.* Some things can never be made simple.
10. *The One.* Simplicity is about subtracting the obvious, and adding the meaningful.

Having a system for reducing the complex down to simpler thinking is central to getting things done, and we will use some of this thinking as inspiration when we get down to the business of writing good lists. There is a summary of the book in the Appendix. In essence though, the laws suggest that, in order to successfully *Tick Achieve*, you should:

- Reduce what you have to do to the simplest possible action.
- Get organized.
- Be efficient with your time.

- Learn what works and constantly make refinements.
- Don't try to be simplistic about things that really are complicated.

> *"We must strive to meet that simplicity that lies beyond sophistication."*
>
> **John Gardner**

How eliminating issues gets to faster answers

The important point here is that the more you can eliminate, the easier it is to get things done, which is the purpose of this book. This could have a number of benefits, and the importance of these will vary depending on what is important to you. Possible benefits of leaving it out are:

Clarity:	can see what needs doing
Priority:	get the important things done first
Progress:	nothing at all was getting done before
Speed:	do everything else faster
Volume:	get more done in total

It is hard to generalize, but you should be able to equate which set of benefits are most helpful to you. It is then a simple matter to convert these possible outcomes into a small set of precursor questions to determine your preference.

- Can I see what needs doing?
- What tasks are the most important and so should be done first?
- Which task will create the greatest feeling of progress?
- What tasks can be done fastest, or very quickly?

You can begin to see here that personal psychology starts to enter into it. Are you the sort of person who would rather do one large, important item, or lots of little ones? There is no right or wrong answer, but ultimately you need to be able to do both, so long as you understand the tasks that you will tend to avoid. Then we can put tripwires in place to make sure you do the ones that you like least and will continue to put off (see Chapter 7: *Outthink yourself*).

These early questions form the basis of our set of Killer Questions, which will ultimately provide you with the definitive checklist for getting things done. But before we move on, we have to wrestle with the big one, which is:

Does this need to be done at all?

Extraneous extraction

I said at the beginning of this chapter that skilful editing and the ability to filter out extraneous material is a crucial asset for anyone who wants to *Tick Achieve* effectively. Now let's determine the principles of extraneous extraction. This is what extraneous can mean:

Extraneous:
1. not essential
2. not pertinent or applicable; irrelevant
3. coming from without
4. not belonging; unrelated to that to which it is added

So now we can add to our store of Killer Questions:

• Is this task essential?
• Is this task pertinent, applicable or relevant?
• Does this task come from without?
• Is this task unrelated to the matter in hand?

What all this basically means is that, if the proposed task is not essential, then you probably shouldn't do it. I am not proposing that you strip out everything in your life not based on basic subsistence, but I am suggesting that you subject most tasks to this line of questioning. It will only take you a couple of seconds, and it could save you hours on each occasion.

How leaving it out forces the issue

Leave it out, or even consider leaving it out, and you force the issue. John Maeda highlights this point by asking pairs of questions.

"How simple can you make it? vs. How complex does it have to be?"

> *"The absence of alternatives clears the mind marvellously."*
>
> **Henry Kissinger, quoted in The New York Times**

We live in an age where people are loath to admit that something can be done simply, as well as effectively. Why not just admit that something is easy to get done, and then do it?

"How can you make the wait shorter? vs. How can you make the wait more tolerable?"

If you know there is likely to be a delay in the completion of a task, and that may cause you some anxiety, then consider how to make the wait more bearable.

"How directed can I stand to feel? vs. How direction-less can I afford to be?"

Lack of direction can be horrible, and much of it is self-inflicted. And yet many of us resent control. Determine the balance you find acceptable, and self-impose it.

Reductionism: think harder and simplify everything

In philosophy, reductionism is a theory that claims that the nature of complex things is reduced to the nature of sums of simpler or more fundamental things. This could be said of objects, phenomena, explanations, theories, and so on.

Reductionism is sometimes believed to suggest the unity of science. For example, fundamental chemistry is based on physics, fundamental biology and geology are based on chemistry, psychology is based on biology, and so on. Some of these reductions are commonly accepted, but others are controversial because there are those who claim that complex systems are inherently irreducible or holistic.

If you want to get things done, you have to embrace the broad idea behind reductionism. The reason for this is that, if you always view things holistically, the task will almost always seem too big and daunting. You have to be able to see the constituent parts, and break it all down into manageable chunks. It helps if you have a boxy mind, or if you can train yourself to adopt one.

Boxy minds and why they help

What is a boxy mind? It is a phrase that I have invented to describe people who have the ability to bundle up different tasks and problems so that they can approach them in the right way. To understand how this might work, we need to glance quickly at the world of psychology. Ulric Neisser is generally regarded as "The Father of Cognitive Psychology". In his 1967 book he defined cognition as the *"processes by which the sensory input is transformed, reduced, elaborated, stored, recovered and used . . . cognition is involved in everything a human being might possibly do"*. The brain is often described as a computer, but the use of metaphors such as this has a long history. In the 17th century, for example, brains were described as clocks. In other words, whatever is the latest technology tends to be used. Using the computer metaphor for now, the brain provides the hardware and thoughts (usually manifesting themselves as some form of language) provide the software. It is then possible to isolate:

• Inputs (auditory, sensory and visual).
• Outputs (motor).
• Data processing.
• Memory (general, motor).

I have no desire to over-complicate this. If you find it an interesting area, then you might want to read *Introducing Psychology* by Nigel Benson. Suffice to say, the experts have accurately identified which parts of the brain do what, and with a bit of discipline you can do the same, metaphorically. Imagine your mind as a picture of a phrenologist's head. Imagine drawing on it various categories of task that need doing. By putting the right task in the right box, you are halfway to getting things done in the right order with the right degree of urgency. That's the power of a boxy mind. We will return to this idea in Chapter 5, when we look at how to write good lists. But first we need to understand the idea of anti lists.

Anti lists

I briefly introduced this idea in a previous book, *So What?* Now is the time to develop the idea much more fully. An anti list is a list of what you are *not* going to do. This is a crucial aid to establishing what you *are* going to do. There are various ways in which writing this list can really help. It establishes:

1. What you will *never* do.
2. What you don't *want* to do.
3. What you won't do *today*.
4. What action really *will* help achieve the task.

All are tremendously helpful to know, and could be equally valid, depending on the task. Firstly, it is crucial to know what you will never do. Whatever these things are, they are vital components of your standards, principles and personal character. If you have never done the exercise before, take a sheet of paper, write at the top "I will never . . ." and fill it in. It's a very therapeutic process. One small point though: if you have written this down then you must stick to it otherwise you will hate yourself. Completing this sentence is part of your one-page personal plan. If you want to complete the whole thing now, go to Chapter 10 and look at Figure 10.1.

Secondly, you will clarify what you do and don't want to do. We all have to do things that we don't really want to, and obviously some are much worse than others. Paying the gas bill isn't much fun, but it's nothing when it comes to ringing someone and telling them a friend has died. It's all relative. Identifying what you don't want to do, versus what you will never do, is a very helpful comparison.

The third point, what you won't do today, is a temporal one, and one of priority. Prevaricators, who make a life's work out of putting everything off, require significant help here.

Tasks do not improve in quality if they are delayed.

The value of establishing what you won't do today is so that you can do more important things first, not so that you never do them. Also, today is just one unit of time to describe when the task will be done. It could equally apply to:

- In the next five minutes.
- In the next hour.
- This morning.
- Tomorrow.
- This week.
- This month.
- This year.

Don't become a victim of time. You must be acutely aware that the longer the unit of time, the less likely it is that the task will be done. We will discuss this more later. For the moment though, stick to the principle of reducing what you have to do.

Do less and get more done.

Towards a manifesto for *Tick Achieve*

All of this is heading towards something of a mini-manifesto for those who wish to *Tick Achieve*. It looks something like this:

1. **Say no more often.**
2. **Debate hard and early.**
3. **Have a system.**

4. **Trust your Depth Mind.**
5. **Kick bad habits.**

Let's work through each in turn.

Say no more often

There are lots of ways to say no, but before we get into those, let me clarify something important: aggression never works. Genuine concern to get it right usually does. I am not advocating simply refusing to do anything you are asked to do, whether that is at work, at home, or socially. That's not going to get you anywhere. But what I am proposing is that you become much more inquisitive so that you don't blindly accept whatever you are told to do without believing it to be a good and useful action.

Here are some ways to say no politely:

> *"The consequences of doing what you suggest are x and y* (something not good or helpful). *Are you still sure about this?"*

Let them consider and give them time to think. They may well withdraw the idea once they have heard your opinion. This can be particularly helpful if the person in question respects your opinion. This is a direct example of applying the *"If I do x, then y will happen"* principle we discussed in Chapter 1.

> *"I really wouldn't recommend this. It goes against all my previous experience."*

Obviously you need to be reasonably experienced to pull this one off, but it does work when you know you are respected by the other person, and is particularly important if you are part of a team.

"I really don't agree because of reasons x, y, z."

This is a purely rational response, and can be deployed when you have a good understanding of a subject and all the issues. Try to keep it unemotional, and let the facts speak for themselves. If they are sufficiently strong, then you won't have to push the point.

"May I discuss this with a colleague and call you back?"

This is admittedly a case of stalling for time, but it is valid. Many people who ask for something either forget or change their mind by the following day. By building in thinking time, you take the edge off confrontation and allow for a more considered response at a later point.

"I have already discussed that possibility and rejected it as inappropriate for the following reasons."

A lot of people are very inconsistent. Sometimes a new request flies in the face of what has been discussed before, and it is often appropriate to remind them of important discussions that have already taken place. Recap on any previous conversations, meetings and discussions that have a bearing on the outcome.

"I want this to be really carefully thought through. Can I think about it and discuss it with you tomorrow?"

In many walks of life, a solution that takes longer is valued more, whereas the immediate response is regarded as too spontaneous to be well considered. If this is true in your area, then you need to understand the value of retiring to think. It also buys you some time and gives you the chance to seek advice if you want to.

"It would be really helpful to understand what has changed because we agreed this yesterday."

It is amazing the number of times when you think something is agreed and then suddenly it isn't. Even stranger, the person delivering the news often makes no mention of what has changed and what the reasons are. In these circumstances, it is your job to ask the question. It is only reasonable that, if you are being asked to do something new, you should be told why. If you disapprove of the new direction, then say: *"Mmm, this sheds a different light on things. May I have time to consider?"*

There are also plenty of rather more devious approaches to saying no. I don't necessarily approve, but they can be amusing. Here are my favourites that have emerged from people attending my training over the last few years:

1. Confuse the issue by continually introducing new considerations until they have forgotten their original request.
2. Say yes. Then find a way of saying no later.
3. Treat it as a request for further information.

Debate hard and early

All of these ways of saying no are a type of tough love. To reduce the amount of irrelevant things that you have to do, you have to learn how to apply them and stick up for yourself. Robust debate is another crucial part of the process. If you passively accept everything you are told to do, then you aren't going to have a very interesting or fulfilling job. Given that over half the jobs available now are in service industries, do bear in mind that many people are hired for their opinion. So don't be shy about expressing yours. If you think a proposal is daft, then say so. Obviously you need to back your argument up, and a slanging match is no way to progress. Try to do this early on so that time isn't so much of an issue. There's nothing worse than someone saying nothing, doing the job, and then saying afterwards that they thought it was a poor idea all along.

Have a system

We will devise a full system when we look at how to write the ultimate list, but here we want to establish the basic principle that some sort of system is a desirable thing. If you don't concoct an organizational system, you are unlikely to get much done. I am not suggesting that you become robotic, but if you choose not to have a system then you won't know where anything is, what order to do things in, or where to start. Or at least, you will be leaving the execution of all the things that matter to chance, and that is the opposite of what this book wants to help you achieve.

John Maeda suggests various systems. The two most helpful in the context of *Tick Achieve* are:

SHE: Shrink, Hide, Embody

SLIP: Sort, Label, Integrate, Prioritize

Shrink means you should make every reference and feature of your system as small and pithy as possible. Hide means that as little should be on view as possible – only what you need at that precise moment. Embody is a broader concept – efficiency should be built in from the start, regardless of whether it is obviously on display. SLIP is easier to explain: you need to sort your tasks, label them in some way, integrate them into your programme of activity, and give them priority (I am not a fan of the word prioritize).

Having some kind of system obviously means that you need to write down ideas and tasks so that you won't forget them. There is nothing revolutionary about this idea, but there is a crucial point that many people fail to appreciate:

Once you have written a task down you can forget about it.

It is extraordinary the number of people who continue fretting about something they have already made a note to do. At this stage, assuming they have a decent system, they can stop thinking about it. That's the whole point of having a system.

> *"Never write when you can speak. Never speak when you can nod."*
>
> **Martin Lomasney, quoted in The Nation**

Trust your Depth Mind

In his excellent book *The Art of Creative Thinking*, John Adair urges us to make better use of our *Depth Mind*. *Depth Mind* is his term for what many of us would refer to as our subconscious. The overriding concern with our subconscious, however, is that we don't understand it well and believe we have no control over it. This may well be true, but it doesn't mean that it can't do useful work. Adair proposes that you trust your subconscious to sort things out and generate solutions once you have "briefed it". He uses the metaphor of a submarine at sea to illustrate that thinking can sometimes leave the surface and proceed on its voyage many fathoms below. Then it can surface again into the conscious mind. There is a summary of this thinking in the Appendix.

What has all this got to do with getting things done? Well, many of our tasks are not short-term things that can be rattled off in a couple of minutes. They require proper consideration. But when there are hundreds of other things to do, they often do not receive decent consideration time. This is where you should trust your *Depth Mind* more. With an effective system, you can "brief" your mind to consider the issue, and put a reminder in for a later date when you need to progress it. A good system can also make good ideas come back to you when needed. We will look at how to do this in the next couple of chapters.

Kick bad habits

And finally, you do of course have to throw out all your old bad habits. If you are honest with yourself, you will know instinctively what these are, but here are some possibilities:

1. Having no system at all.
2. Having a system of sorts, but one that doesn't work very well.
3. Mixing several systems together ineffectively.
4. Prejudging what you think will be nice things to do.
5. Putting off what you think will be nasty tasks.
6. Delaying anything complicated.
7. Being highly efficient one day, and totally ineffective the next.
8. Continually putting things you don't want to do to the bottom of the list.
9. Concentrating more on the list than the tasks on it.
10. Never getting anything done because you keep rewriting your list.

All of these bad habits will have to go.

Killer Questions

This chapter has covered quite a few possible laws to help you get things done, and raised a lot of questions that help you to filter out the irrelevant. There are twenty-four in total, and I have kept them in the groups in which they arose:

1. Can I see what needs doing?
2. What tasks are the most important and so should be done first?
3. Which task will create the greatest feeling of progress?
4. What tasks can be done fastest, or very quickly?

5. Have you reduced what you have to do to the simplest possible action?
6. Are you well organized?
7. Is this the most efficient use of your time?
8. What can you learn from what works well?
9. What refinements can be made to your system?
10. Have you been overly simplistic about things that really are complicated?

11. Is this task essential?
12. Is this task pertinent, applicable or relevant?
13. Does this task come from without?
14. Is this task unrelated to the matter in hand?

15. How simple can you make it?
16. How complex does it have to be?
17. How can you make the wait shorter?
18. How can you make the wait more tolerable?
19. How directed can I stand to feel?
20. How directionless can I afford to be?

21. What will you *never* do?

22. What don't you *want* to do?
23. What won't you do *today?*
24. What action will really help to achieve the task?

These should be your first port of call whenever you are deciding whether to do something. You won't use them all at the same time, but you will want to use at least four or five for each task. This will prevent irrelevant tasks slipping through and making their way onto your action list.

How to leave it out

So to summarize what we have covered in this chapter:

- Brevity equals intelligence – do not be tempted to spend any longer on anything than is actually needed to get it done.
- Less really is more – don't assume that the simple route is inadequate, because it takes a confident person to admit that things are often simpler than they at first appear.
- The Laws of Simplicity can help you to strip away unhelpful clutter and get right to the heart of any task.
- Eliminating issues gets to faster answers, so throw out everything that isn't directly relevant to the task in hand.
- To avoid any doubt, invoke the power of the question: does this need to be done at all?
- Extract everything extraneous from your task list.
- Force the issue by considering what would happen if you left it out.
- Think harder and simplify everything.
- Try to adopt the qualities of a boxy mind.
- Draw up an anti list – a list of what you are *not* going to do.
- Tasks do not improve in quality if they are delayed.
- Work out how to do less and you will get more done.

- Say no more often – you will end up with less to do.
- Debate hard and early, and never do anything you think is a bad idea.
- Have a system and stick to it.
- Once you have written a task down you can forget about it.
- Trust your Depth Mind to keep working once you have "briefed" it.
- Kick your old bad habits.

One in a Row

4

"Think positive — you never know what you can't do till you can't do it".

This chapter covers why achievement does not have to be a relentless series of successes. Breaking big problems down and celebrating mini steps. Rapid Sequential Tasking and the one-touch approach. Never touch a piece of paper or email more than once. How an untidy desk used to betray disorganization – now technology hides it. Think, do and possible interpretations of it. Improving your time management. The curse of modern technology, managing machines and why most of the people on any given street are moving without paying attention. Attention deficit syndrome: if you want to get something done, turn off your mobile or hand-held device. The overnight test. Why emailed does not mean the job is done. Compress, excess and success. Outline of how to practice one in a row.

Achievement does not have to be a relentless series of successes.

The sublime accountant

Now is the time to pick up the thread of what we discussed in the first chapter: what exactly do we mean by achievement? In the context of *Tick Achieve*, the definition of achieve is not grand. It does not mean becoming Prime Minister, appearing on television or winning the lottery. In my book, it means tiny little achievements that could be as mundane as remembering someone's birthday, not forgetting the milk or delivering a proposal when you said you would. The crucial point is that all these things happen on time without you having a panic or being prompted.

I once had to give a talk in Kent and afterwards I was approached by a guy brandishing a copy of one of my books. He said he was an accountant and had enjoyed reading it. I couldn't help noticing that the book had scores of Post-It notes poking out of it, in what seemed to be some colour-coding system. I just had to ask him what his system was.

"Ah," he said, "green is for good, blue is for brilliant . . ."
"And the pink?"

"Pink is for sublime," he said triumphantly, revealing that inside all the relevant points were highlighted in the correct colour with a ruler. Unlike many who find the big picture too daunting, he had taken one of the most important steps towards becoming a brilliant *Tick Achiever.* He had broken the whole down into small, manageable pieces – a system that worked for him.

> *"The big picture is more likely to paralyse than inspire."*
>
> **Matthew Parris, quoted in The Times**

Breaking big problems down

Stare at a pyramid and you may be inclined to wonder how on earth it was built, particularly in the absence of modern machinery. How did they get the massive *moai* on Easter Island from the quarry to their platforms, and how did they get them to stand upright? The answers are: (a) by using logs as a rolling transport base and (b) by heaving with ropes on one side and inserting stones underneath the other. Gradually the job gets done, and this is the key to *Tick Achieve.* Do not view anything as one enormous task that could frighten the life out of you. View it as a series of small tasks, each perfectly doable in their own right. This approach really works.

How to eat an elephant

Old joke:

"How do you eat an elephant?"
"One mouthful at a time."

Every now and again you read strange stories in the tabloids about some bloke from China who is systematically eating a tractor, or some such oddity. No matter how seemingly impossible, in theory it can be done if you do it a step at a time. The principle holds good. If you want to make something less daunting, or you need to tackle something large, then break it into small pieces, and knock them down one at a time.

Introducing mini steps

In a previous book, *Start*, I introduced the idea of one in a row, and now is the time to expand the theme. It is my firm belief that you don't have to have loads of triumphs all at the same time, or in a blistering sequence, to get things done effectively. Those who have not mastered the art of *Tick Achieve* fail to celebrate each small step or achievement as they go along, and thus remain as paralysed by the overall job as they were at the beginning.

To me, achieving one small thing is a reason for celebration in its own right. Hence the expression: one in a row. The sequence should be *achieve/tick/achieve/tick/achieve/tick*, allowing you the chance to enjoy forward motion each time you take a small step. Should you choose not to do this, you will remain in the old rut of *achieve/worry/achieve/worry/achieve/worry*. Being able to celebrate the success of mini steps on the way is a vital part of staying sane and relentlessly enthusiastic, and is a great force field against motivation crises.

Making progress gradually is a highly desirable thing. It gives you time to absorb the consequences of the achievement, and work out what to do next. Mini steps are crucial to the spirit of *Tick Achieve*. Every epic journey has to start with a first step. Take one mini step and you can shout: *"One in a row!"*

> *"The man who moves a mountain begins by carrying away small stones."*
>
> **Chinese proverb**

Rapid Sequential Tasking

A couple of years ago I had just put the bread in the toaster when my partner asked me a question about holiday plans. *"I'll think about that in a minute"*, I replied, *"I'm just making toast"*. I wasn't joking. It's classic male stuff – we can only do one thing at once apparently. The debate rages on to the point of cliché – women can multitask and men can't. As a male myself I am happy to concede the point: I am not good at doing several things at the same time. So what can a man do if that is truly the case? How can he be any good at getting lots of stuff done all at once?

The secret to me lies in *Rapid Sequential Tasking*. Just because men can't do lots at the same time does not mean that we can't do lots in a sequence, and fast. This is how I tackle the problem of the *"Don't talk to me, I'm making toast"* syndrome. Do things fast, one after the other. It works for me. It also has one distinct advantage over multitasking. There is a strong suspicion that in the case of much multitasking, all the tasks may well have been started, but they may not have been finished. This is a crucial point. Although the beginning of any task is clearly vital, it isn't over until it's over. The beauty of *Rapid Sequential Tasking* is that you don't move on to the next thing until you have finished the last one, thus hugely increasing your ability to *Tick Achieve*.

Neuroscientists, psychologists and management professors suggest that many people would be wise to curb their multitasking behaviour when working in an office, studying or driving a car. The *New York Times* (1 April 2007) concluded that *"one task at a time is probably most efficient"*. Ring any bells with one in a row?

A word here on the sorts of character traits that you need to have or develop in order to become truly successful at getting things done. Those of you who have ever had to fill in a personality assessment when looking for a new job may be familiar with some of the types they identify. The Belbin system, for example (developed by Dr Meredith Belbin), identifies nine team role descriptions, which are:

1. Plant
2. Resource investigator
3. Co-ordinator
4. Shaper
5. Monitor Evaluator
6. Teamworker
7. Implementer
8. Completer Finisher
9. Specialist

Without going into huge detail, the qualities you need in order to *Tick Achieve* effectively are broadly those of the Plant, the Implementer and the Completer Finisher. These are:

Plant: creative, imaginative, unorthodox. Solves difficult problems.
Implementer: disciplined, reliable, conservative and efficient. Turns ideas into practical actions.
Completer Finisher: painstaking, conscientious, anxious. Searches out errors and omissions. Delivers on time.

If you are interested, you can find out more about it at *www.belbin.com.* Naturally, not every single one of these qualities is desirable, and no one is really suggesting that all these qualities should necessarily reside in the same person, because this is a teamwork system. However, for the record, here is my profile of the perfect *Tick Achiever*:

Delivers on time

Imaginative

Reliable

Efficient

Conscientious

Turns ideas into practical actions

Solves difficult problems

For those of you who enjoy mnemonics and acronyms, you will have noticed that this profile spells DIRECTS, which is precisely what you need to do to get everything done effectively.

The one-touch approach

An essential element of the one in a row principle is the one-touch approach. You may have heard of it, and it really works. The basic rule is:

Never touch a piece of paper or email more than once.

This may sound harsh and in some cases almost impossible, but I can assure you it works. The sequence you should follow is:

1. READ IT
2. ACTION IT or FILE IT or BIN IT

Let's work through these permutations. Clearly you need to read it to understand what it is. You then have three options: action, file or bin. If it is a simple task, do it now, and delete the email or throw the piece of paper away (sorry, recycle it). If it needs doing but is more complicated, then make a note of when to do it, and file it in the right place, electronically or physically. If you understand it easily, know it already, if it is irrelevant, or just plain nonsense, then delete it immediately or recycle it. With this simple approach, you will only have immediate action in your in-tray, and you will have a clear understanding of what you are supposed to be doing at any given moment.

When I propose this in training, I sometimes find that sceptics say they couldn't possibly delete their emails in this way. Let me clarify. I fully understand that emails are the new *lingua franca*. Email trails are used to prove that something was asked for, approved, disputed, took a change of direction, and so on. If it is essential in your job to keep these then by all means do, but make sure that you *file them somewhere else*. For example, have a file for approval of budgets, or a correspondence trail of a particularly fraught and lengthy project. Do not leave these messages in your in-box. They will prevent you from being able to *Tick Achieve* everything else that you need to get done.

One of the great unmentioned deceptions of modern business is that you can't physically see if someone is disorganized. You used to be able to spot this from the chaos of papers and files on someone's desk, and in many cases the "untidy desk, untidy mind" principle held good. Now, nobody can see that you have 2000 messages, many of them unanswered, sitting in your in-box. Figures of this size are not uncommon. Most people I ask in training say they have at least a few hundred messages, and the highest I have heard of is 60,000. In extreme cases, some of these people have to come in at the weekend specifically to clear their email in-box. Don't let things pile up like this – it won't happen if you adopt the one-touch approach and celebrate the one in a row idea. So remember:

An untidy desk used to betray disorganization – now technology hides it.

Think, do

Think, do is a related approach that works well in many contexts. As with all the best ideas, it is simple. If you think of something, then do it immediately. This notion is, of course, easy to gainsay. The classic response is: *"I can't do it on the spot because I am doing something else."* This retort doesn't really hold water. It just means that the person rejecting the idea hasn't thought hard enough about what the "do" element of the phrase means. Let's look at this.

Possible meanings of think

1. It is a complicated problem, so it requires a long think.
2. I just thought of it, and I know what to do.

If using the first example, then there is nothing to do until a course of action is determined. Once you have decided what to do, then you can do it. In the second type, you instinctively know what to do, so it's just a question of whether you can do it right now. So what might "do" mean?

Possible meanings of do

1. A simple action that I can do right now.
2. Something more complex, which I can initiate now.
3. Something I cannot do now because it is inconvenient, but I can write it down, which is doing something in its own right.

This is where the interpretation of "do" becomes important. Those who practice this approach are not saying that you can physically do every action the moment you think of it. But the very act of writing down what needs to be done is a doing action that ensures that the job *will* get done, even though you cannot do it at that precise moment. In their book *See, Feel, Think, Do*, Andy Milligan and Shaun Smith have developed this idea a stage further. Think, Do is preceded by See (experience it for yourself) and Feel (empathize with your subject). Then you can move on to Think and Do. The basic point is that instinct is much more powerful than over-reliance on research or data, which can only provide you with a rear-view mirror picture of what happened. The spirit of this suits those who want to *Tick Achieve*. If you sit around analysing something for too long then you may suffer from paralysis by analysis. Your first instinct about how to get something done is usually right. Trust that instinct and get on with it. There is a summary of the book in the Appendix, and we will pursue the instinct theme more in the next chapter.

Improving your time management

> *"Accomplishing the impossible means only that your boss will add it to your regular duties."*
>
> **Larson**

It's a dilemma, isn't it? If you work for someone else, the more you do, the more you get given to do. It's a seemingly never-ending cycle. However, if you are efficient, then what an asset that could be in your private life, or if you work for yourself. So whilst I accept that you don't want to bring an endless stream of tasks onto your desk, the main aspects of getting things done remain desirable capabilities to have. Here are some ideas for improving your time management. It's my SMOG plan, designed to remove the pollution from your average working day:

1. **S**et aside planning time.
2. **M**ake meetings shorter.
3. **O**rganize yourself.
4. **G**et your attitude right.

Set aside planning time

- Allow thinking time for you to come up with new ideas.
- Build in leisure and relaxation time, so include the spare-time hours not just the working ones.
- This means planning sleep, exercise and relaxation, as well as work.
- Set aside fixed and limited amounts of time to return phone calls and answer emails – then get on with what needs to be done.

Make meetings shorter

- Wherever possible, question whether a meeting is really necessary at all.
- Prepare properly for meetings so that they can be finished more quickly.
- Make presentations and proposals shorter.
- Never be late. Allow plenty of time and, if you are early, use the time to think.
- Use travelling time as thinking time.
- Make phone calls shorter and come to the point without being terse.

(See Chapter 9 for a complete list of how to liven up meetings.)

Organize yourself

- Write everything down, cross things off when you have done them, and keep your list right up to date.
- Type out a list of things to do and people to call. Print it out. If it is on screen you won't do it.
- Work out the time lag between when you start something and when you will have achieved what you need – then plan for it.

Get your attitude right

- Always finish the day by deciding what to do the next day.
- Never do anything unless you know why you are doing it – only do the things that matter.
- Do not draw a distinction between nice and nasty things to do – frequently the outcome is the opposite of what you expect.
- Do not delay doing the things you don't like – get them out of the way.

- Be more decisive – don't delay decisions unless they need very careful thought or consultation with someone else.
- If you think it, do it.

So next time you want to clear the air, use the SMOG plan.

"Time flies over us, but leaves its shadows behind."

Nathaniel Hawthorne

The curse of modern technology

No book on how to get things done would be complete without some reference to modern technology. Don't get me wrong: there are hundreds of things that are excellent about modern gadgets, and as a sole trader I am more than grateful for the many wonderful things they enable me to achieve. However, there are very few places where anyone can go to receive advice on how to cope with the effects of technology and, to my knowledge, no one ever gets trained in how to control the stuff. I don't mean how to work your way round a complicated software user interface. I mean living a calm life, getting a lot done on the one hand, whilst on the other not being constantly harassed and stressed because of persistent intrusions facilitated by the very technology that is designed to make your life easier.

"I have developed a new philosophy – only dread one day at a time."

Charlie Brown

Managing machines

A lot of studies have been conducted recently into the difficulty people have in managing their machines. They all conclude that multitasking with all these devices actually slows you down, and in some cases the level of distraction can be fatal. Every year over a dozen teenagers in Britain are killed because they stroll across the road without looking whilst texting on a mobile phone or listening to an iPod. In a tragic recent case, a teenage driver was sent to jail because she killed a pedestrian whilst simultaneously driving at 70 mph and sending a text. Everywhere you go you now see people bumping into each other in the street because they are looking at a mobile or hand-held device rather than where they are going. Cyclists who listen to music are lethal because they can hear no traffic. Those listening to music whilst walking are blissfully unaware of the movements of others. In short:

Most of the people on any given street are moving without paying attention.

This also has a bearing on office behaviour, and anyone's ability to get things done. In a recent study, a group of Microsoft workers took, on average, fifteen minutes to return to serious mental tasks, like writing reports or computer code, after responding to incoming email or instant messages. They strayed off to reply to other messages or browse news, sports or entertainment websites (*New York Times*, 1 April 2007). The gist of all this is that we are not very adept at managing our machines.

Attention deficit syndrome

With so many devices intruding on our lives all the time, it is worth posing the question: at any given moment, what exactly is anybody concentrating on? Let's look at the main culprits: computers, hand-held devices and mobile phones. Of course all this technology is converging, but the intrusive effects of it can be mapped in broad terms. At work, or if you choose to sit at your desk at home, the computer can prove a distraction for hours. Disregarding computer games and incessant surfing and Googling (both of which have split up many a marriage), there will be incoming email. As I write, my daily SPAM count is between fifty and a hundred. This I delete without looking at, but some don't. There are three critical rules in coping with email:

1. Look at SPAM once, and unsubscribe from everything unwanted.
2. Never have a noise that alerts you to incoming mail.
3. Only look at emails at specific times that you choose.

Hand-held devices are, in the main, a personal disaster. Let me explain. In the same way that we all have a devil in us that could slide into alcoholism or some dependency, we all crave attention. These devices provide that attention. The more weak-willed people are, the more they need their machine to prove they are in demand.

CrackBerry n: a person who obsessively uses their BlackBerry (*from Ducks in a Row, An A–Z of Offlish, Carl Newbrook*)

Unable to distinguish between a social or a work message, these obsessives wreck their home lives by constantly checking who has been in touch. There is also a whole generation of people who go into meetings, pretend to pay attention, but actually keep checking messages under the table. These are not just the workaholics we discussed earlier, but also people who believe that the world cannot function without them. They are sorely deluded, and are missing the point:

If you want to get something done, turn off your mobile or hand-held device.

As an amusing side note, my friend and author Jon Steel became so agitated by the intrusion of his machine that he deliberately drove over it with his car. Sad to report, the damn thing didn't break. It wasn't until he borrowed his neighbour Trevor's sledgehammer that he could finally silence it. For the full account of this, and a whimsical accompanying photograph, buy a copy of *Perfect Pitch* by Jon Steel.

Mobiles can be just as bad. I never turn mine on in the morning until I am ready, which often isn't until 11am. If there are messages, then I attend to them. You need only check twice a day if you are busy. A lot of people these days have no watch or alarm clock, so they leave their mobiles on all night. Drunk friends may well call in the small hours. They get no peace.

Hello Personal Organizer, goodbye Personal Assistant

Another effect of the onslaught of technology is the demise of the secretary or personal assistant. It started quite gently in the early nineties with the arrival of computers. Bosses had to go on courses to master the basics, but they still delegated the typing of the presentations. If you have an electronic diary on your screen, why not fill it in yourself? Then email came in, and people were communicating directly. The money men looked at the payroll and threw out all the secretaries as being unnecessary.

But as well as being a brilliant additional resource, secretaries and personal assistants provided a much more subtle service that most businesses now lack entirely; they screened their boss's instructions for appropriateness. As increasingly stressed bosses fired off instruction after instruction, they provided a safety blanket. *Are you sure you want to phrase it like that? Shall I tone that down a little? I'll just get Richard's advice before I send that.* Many a calamity was undoubtedly saved in this way.

The overnight test

It doesn't happen any more. Everything is of the moment, and always frantically urgent, although it is amusing how many desperately urgent projects are strangely delayed on the whim of a boss somewhere up the line.

The overnight test is always a good idea, particularly in relation to tricky issues. This is also where your Depth Mind can really stand you in good stead. (Look back to Chapter 3 if you have dipped in and want to know more about it.)

Haste and regret

Haste is brilliant if the task is straightforward and risk-free. The rest of the time, it usually leads to regret. I worked with a guy who opened an email from his director saying that a client wouldn't pay a bill for £70,000. The recipient described the client as a four-letter word and hit reply. He had in fact hit "reply all", which promptly sent it to the client as well. Two minutes later, the client replied to the effect that, given what the agency thought of them, they certainly would not be paying the bill.

> *"Pray, verb: to ask that the laws of the universe be temporarily annulled for a single petitioner, confessedly unworthy."*
>
> **Ambrose Pierce**

There are many morals to be learned from the way in which much modern technology is used. The most important are:

1. Think hard about how you want it to affect your life.
2. Make it work for you, not the other way round.
3. Only turn it on for specific times each day.
4. Turn it off when you need to get things done.
5. Don't assume you can handle it all at once.
6. Don't hide behind it.
7. Don't let it lure you into doing inappropriate things.
8. Do not let it come between you and those you care about.
9. Do not confuse what it can do with tasks that require humanity.
10. Do not assume that any job is done by the technology alone.

My final point on this is one of delegation:

Emailed does not mean the job is done.

Some people seem to think that once they have fired off an email, they can wash their hands of something. Nothing could be further from the truth. Among the possible reasons for this are:

1. The email never arrives.
2. The intended recipient never reads it.
3. They are not there.
4. They are too busy or disorganized.
5. They read it, but they don't agree.
6. They want to discuss it with you first.

Try talking to people – it is much more charming, and almost always more effective.

Compress, excess and success

My summary mantra for leave it out and one in a row is: compress, excess, success. Compress all your tasks down to the smallest number by questioning everything and determining a clear purpose and cause and effect. Understand what action will lead to the outcome you desire. Get rid of all the excess baggage that does not serve the purpose. Don't be sheepish about this: the fewer the tasks, the more in total you will get done. Celebrate the mini steps that make progress: one in a row. All of which will lead to success in the constant struggle to *Tick Achieve*.

> *"To err is human, but to really foul things up you need a computer."*
>
> **Paul Ehrlich, quoted in The Boston Globe**

How to practice one in a row

So to summarize the points in this chapter:

- Achievement does not have to be a relentless series of successes – celebrate the value of one in a row every time.
- Break big problems down into small, manageable chunks so that you can see the simplicity of the constituent parts.
- Use mini steps to wrestle with big problems, otherwise you will become overwhelmed by the apparent enormity of what is ahead.
- Don't worry about multitasking – consider Rapid Sequential Tasking instead.
- Use the one-touch approach to avoid wasting time when dealing with paper work and emails.

- When you think of something, do it straightaway if possible, or write it down immediately if you can't.
- Improve your time management by setting aside planning time, making meetings shorter, organizing yourself and getting your attitude right.
- Pay careful attention to the manner in which you use modern technology.
- Compress your tasks, remove the excess and celebrate small successes.

Tick Achieve

5

" Concentrate—that's our credo...
.... Hello Phil, what's up..? "

This chapter covers why to tick off is to move on. The need for structure and how to draw inspiration from boxy minds and phrenologists. The art of great list writing. The PERFECT system: Personal priority, Emotional importance, Reason for doing, Financial value to you, Everyone else's priorities, Chronological sift, Time shifts. VPNs: Vital, Preferable and Nice to have. The Priority Matrix. Bad lists and how to spot them. Don't talk about it, do it: how talk can be the enemy of action. The power of instinct and the views of the experts. Tick Achieve *as a way of life. Just because a task is started, it doesn't mean it is finished – it's only finished when it is finished. Outline of how to* Tick Achieve.

To tick off is to move on.

When it comes down to it, the heart of *Tick Achieve* is to know what you need to do and then do it. It's as simple as that. Or is it simple? Let's just spell that out again:

1. Know what you need to do.
2. Do it.

You wouldn't have thought that it was difficult, and yet people have terrible trouble with it. The two parts are critically linked. If you don't know what you need to do, then clearly you can't do it. Equally though, many people do things without ever establishing the reason first. Neither permutation gets you anywhere, so the thinking part is fundamental to the doing part. For those who find linking these two together difficult (and that is no disgrace), the answer is usually a list of some kind. A list is the vital link piece between knowing what to do and actually doing it. In that respect, you could reframe the two points as three:

1. Know what you need to do.
2. Write a list.
3. Do it.

Why are lists so important? The answer lies in the volume of tasks to be done, and the time lag between establishing their need and actually doing them. The raison d'être of the list is essentially the fallibility of the human memory. The fewer the number of tasks, the less likely the need for a list. If you have three things to do, you won't need a list. But as soon as the number of tasks creeps up, and it will take a while to do them, then the possibility of forgetting becomes an issue. So in this chapter we are going to tackle the essential art of how to write a decent list, so as to maximize your chances of doing everything.

> *"A good plan violently executed right now is far better than a perfect plan executed next week."*
>
> **General George Patton**

The need for structure

A good list has the power to generate order out of seeming chaos. In the main, humans don't like chaos, and certainly not when they are trying to get things done. Order and structure are important to getting things done, but I don't wish to overplay the point. I am not advocating a trainspotterish anally retentive approach (yes, the word trainspotterish is in the dictionary). In fact, the emphasis should be on the speed and efficiency with which all the tasks can be done, thereby liberating you to do all sorts of more interesting things with a free conscience. This need for structure is not an isolated phenomenon. In fact, it lies at the very heart of what we humans require from modern life. Have a look at what Alvin Toffler has to say:

> "... most people surveying the world around them today see only chaos. They suffer a sense of personal powerlessness and pointlessness."

> "Individuals need life structure. A life lacking in comprehensive structure is an aimless wreck. The absence of structure breeds breakdown. Structure provides the relatively fixed points of reference we need."

> "... for many people, a job is crucial psychologically, over and above the paycheck. By making clear demands on their time and energy, it provides an element of structure around which the rest of their lives can be organised."

> **Alvin Toffler, The Third Wave,**
> quoted in *The E Myth Revisited*, Michael E. Gerber

So, in the same way that people crave structure in their lives, they need it at work, and they need it to help them get done the things that matter to them.

Boxy minds and phrenologists

If you are reading the book sequentially, you will recall that in Chapter 3 we had a look at the idea of boxy minds and phrenologists' heads. Phrenology is the branch of science concerned with localization of the functions in the brain. You will have seen pictures of the human head divided into sections, usually with descriptions of which bits do what written on them. This is the image I want you to have in mind when considering the idea of a boxy mind. I want you to be able to envisage different boxes for different tasks, and to develop the discipline to put them there. If you put them in the right place, then they are easier to retrieve, and easier to do.

> *"Whether you think that you can, or that you can't, you are usually right."*
>
> **Henry Ford, quoted in the Palm Beach Post**

The art of great list writing

There are an infinite number of ways to describe and organize these boxes, but all of them are based in some way on the importance to the doer. If it is a personal list, then you will be the sole decider of what is and isn't important. If someone else is making suggestions (this could be your boss, or your partner or children), then it becomes your job to filter their requests with yours. The conflict between the two is often difficult, with many people feeling that they are being pulled in too many directions. This is where it can help to adopt the boxy approach, and turn the whole thing into something of a system. I am pretty sure that it is impossible to devise a universal one that suits everybody. Instead, I propose that you consider the elements of the one I have invented and choose the bits that work for you so that you can effectively design your own.

The PERFECT system

In developing a system, which I call the PERFECT system, I have tried to consider all the possible types of reason why anyone should need to do something, and what the factors might be that could influence their reason for doing one thing before another. They are: factual, emotional, rational, financial, influential, temporal and exclusional. Let's have a look at these in turn.

Factual refers to the facts. X needs to be done and there's no getting away from it. At a certain time I need to get up and go to work. I need to eat at some point today and drink some water. These ones are unavoidable and undeniable.

Emotional is what you feel. X really matters to me. I want to do it, and I may well decide that it is more important than something factual, even though pure common sense would suggest otherwise.

Rational is not quite the same as factual. Based on calm rational thought, X needs doing first.

Financial is the money area. If I don't do X, then I will be penalized by losing money in some way. If I don't pay the parking ticket, the price of it will double. If I don't pay my credit card, the interest will go up even more.

Influential. I know what I would do, but everyone else is trying to get me to do other things. They are claiming that their X is more important than mine. I want to take the day off but my boss says I can't. I want to go on a stag weekend when my wife says I should be looking after the kids.

Temporal. I can see that X needs doing before Y. I am sure that Z can wait until next week. Temporal order is a great ally in the quest for a decent list.

Exclusional. I am going to exclude X because, on reflection, I don't think it needs doing at all. I thought I needed a new suit but frankly I don't.

At one point or another, all these influences are equally valid in determining what you do and when. The problem is that if you let them all remain equal, then you will never establish any order of priority for your list and you will be no better off in your quest to get things done effectively. So in proposing the PERFECT system, I am not saying that you should work through it sequentially and apply all the factors to your decision-making. Instead, it will work better if you scan the possibilities and choose one set of factors as the basis for your decisions. So, for example, if emotion matters more to you than rationality in a particular context, then use emotional criteria to determine in which order you do things. Bear in mind also that you can wear different hats on different days. You may decide to be rational at work, emotional at home, chronological at the weekend, and so on. So let's look more specifically at the system. PERFECT stands for:

Personal priority

Emotional importance

Reason for doing

Financial value to you

Everyone else's priorities

Chronological sift

Time shifts

Now we are going to work through the seven factors. As we go along, begin to think about which style suits you best, and in what contexts. If you conclude that you can see the merit in all of them, then consider how you can blend them into your own system.

Personal priority

For high self-esteem, personal priority should be your first port of call. The best reason in the world for doing something is undoubtedly because you think it is. If you live or work on your own, if you are massively rich or in charge of everybody (why are you reading this book?), or if what you are contemplating has no bearing whatsoever on anybody else, then personal priority is the best way to go. Write everything down on a sheet of paper, randomly as you think of them. When you think you have captured every-thing, go back through the list putting a number by each point. Now rewrite the list in rank order with the most important at the top and, crucially, *do the tasks in that order*. There is no point in assigning an order of priority only to start doing things in the middle of the list.

Emotional importance

Emotional reasons are essential to your peace of mind. The person who only does things for rational reasons will end up driving themselves or everyone else mad. The degree to which emotion is appropriate will, of course, vary hugely depending on the context. There is little point in getting emotional about how to open a tin of beans, but wherever opinion is the central point, emotion holds the key. Work on the principle that you will do the things that matter to you most, first. Write everything that needs doing on a piece of paper, then reorganize it based on your emotional preference.

Reason for doing

Rational reasons can be very powerful. If the answer to the question *"Why do I need to do this?"* is rational, then you may not be able to get away from it. Whilst it will usually be a contradiction to suggest that one reason can be more rational than another, you can still create an order of prior-ity. Write down the tasks, and number them. Then rewrite the list in the new order. If you have trouble generating the order, then consider overlaying other reasons (such as emotional) so as to establish their level of priority. Or read on for other possible criteria.

Financial value to you

There are two types of financial value to you. I stress "to you" because I am not referring to pure monetary value. Just because something is very expensive or highly valuable does not mean it should come first. In fact, in many cases it may be more appropriate if it came way later. The two types I have in mind are:

1. What you stand to gain.
2. What you stand to lose.

If you stand to gain financially by acting quickly, then you should do so. This seems straightforward enough. Also, however, do consider the penalty cost if something is not done. Whilst it is unlikely that every task on a list will have a monetary angle, it may be worth separating out the ones that do, and ranking them according to the potential loss or gain to generate the order in which they should be done.

Everyone else's priorities

This is where the influential part comes in. Influential reasons originate from everyone else's priorities which, it goes without saying, may well not be the same as yours. If you have a large checklist with very varied tasks, then it could well be worth separating out those that you want to do from those that others have asked or told you to do. It's a revealing process. Ideally, there should be significantly more that you have originated than those imposed or requested by others. If it is the other way round, you may wish to rethink your job description, or ask whether you are saying no often enough (see Chapter 3).

Chronological sift

Temporal reasons are one of your greatest assets in drawing up a decent list. A list of twenty things to do could look very daunting on a Monday. But if they were re-expressed as four things to do per day Monday to Friday, then they would all be done by the end of the week without too much difficulty. Sifting tasks chronologically makes life so much easier. Take a piece of paper and organize your tasks chronologically. Then, instead of having one long list of jobs fading away into the future, break it into the days on which they actually need doing. Each day, simply look at the shorter list.

Time shifts

And finally, the exclusional reasons. These are designed to question whether something needs doing at all, or whether they can be significantly shifted in time. The idea is to exclude as much as possible from today's list. The two crucial questions are:

1. Should this be off the list completely and forever?
2. Is this a temporary activity that I can allocate to a specific day?

If the answer to either question is yes, then you have immediately reduced today's burden of work. Reducing the number of tasks remains at the heart of *Tick Achieve*. So to recap on the PERFECT system, you should aim to reorder your tasks using one or more of these criteria:

Personal priority
Emotional importance
Reason for doing
Financial value to you
Everyone else's priorities
Chronological sift
Time shifts

VPNs

If you still can't decide which criterion to use from this list, then it can sometimes help to take the same list of what needs doing, and then reorder it in two different ways for comparison. So, for example, type your list out in any order on your computer, and print it out twice. Write "personal" at the top of one and "financial value" at the top of the other. Rank the tasks on each list by the two different criteria and see what you come up with. This process could highlight that certain tasks have high priority on both dimensions, or that you have been thinking about a task in the wrong context.

Of course, there are lots of other ways to organize your list. Here's another one that I call VPN. In the world of computers, a VPN is a virtual private network that allows communication to be channelled through another network, and dedicated for a specific use. My VPN stands for:

Vital
Preferable
Nice to have (or **N**ot essential)

This really couldn't be simpler. Get out your list and start with the first question:

1. Is it vital? If it is, then by definition it is high priority.
2. Is it preferable that this task gets done? If yes, then these tasks come next, after the vital ones.
3. Is it nice to have, but not essential? If yes, then it can wait, or be planned for the future.

The Priority Matrix

For those of you who prefer a visual approach to sorting out priorities, I can offer a simple graphic system that you can draw up in seconds on any scrap of paper. It is called the Priority Matrix, and was aired in a previous book – So What? (chapter 7).

The Priority Matrix (Figure 5.1) is based on only two variables: importance and urgency. If you prefer a graphic approach, just draw the two lines on a sheet of paper and scribble each task into the relevant segment. If it is urgent and important, do it now. If it is urgent but not important, delegate it, or get it out of the way first. If it is important but

Figure 5.1 The Priority Matrix

not urgent, think about what you need to do and plan ahead. If it is neither important nor urgent, then don't do it. Sometimes all you need to do is work out what is most important and what is most urgent.

Bad lists and how to spot them

We have looked at more than ten different ways to bring priority to your task list: personal reasons, emotional importance, rational reasons, financial value to you, everyone else's priorities, time shifts, whether they are urgent, important, vital, preferable, or just nice to have but not essential. One way or another, one set of these criteria, or a combination of them, should get you organized. Failing that, use a visual approach like the Priority Matrix.

How can you tell a bad list? Here's an example of one:

Pick up kids
Book holiday
Pay gas bill
Sarah's birthday
Dry cleaning
Puncture
Strategy document for VP
Vet
Haircut
Phone charger

What's wrong with it? There is no distinction between whether something is urgent, important, vital, or preferable. There is no clue as to when any of it has to be done. The owner of this list should try to apply some of the ideas in this chapter. If they chose the chronological approach, it might read:

Monday morning: Pay gas bill, collect dry cleaning, fix puncture

Monday afternoon: Buy Sarah's birthday present, pick up kids

Tomorrow: Phone charger

Next week: Strategy document for VP, vet, haircut

Long-term: Book holiday

Everything that is reduced to smaller constituent parts increases your chances of being able to *Tick Achieve*.

Don't talk about it: do it

A quick reminder about strategic waffle and how it can be counterproductive. In Chapter 2 we discussed how there is a general culture of talking about things at the expense of actually doing them. One thing is certain:

Talk can be the enemy of action.

So whenever you are wondering why things aren't getting done, do pause to think whether this is because you are talking about them too much. It may be that you tend to talk too much, or it may be that discussing things with everyone else is the prime reason. It doesn't really matter which it is, the task is still not completed.

> *"The less I say the more my work gets done."*
>
> **Elton John, Philadelphia Freedom**

The power of instinct

Some people feel paralysed in their attempts to *Tick Achieve* by whether they are doing the right thing, or doing it the right way. This is detrimental. Most people would be better served by trusting their instincts implicitly. In his book Blink, Malcolm Gladwell says that our ability to "know" something in a split-second judgement, without really knowing why we know, is one of the most powerful abilities we possess. A snap judgement made very quickly can actually be far more effective than one we make deliberately and cautiously.

By blocking out what is irrelevant and focusing on narrow slices of experience, we can read seemingly complex situations in the blink of an eye. This is essentially "thinking without thinking". He introduces the theory of "thin slicing" – using the first two seconds of any encounter to determine intuitively your response or the likely outcome. He demonstrates that this "little bit of knowledge" can go a long way, and is accurate in over 80% of instances.

He goes on to show that, strangely, it is possible to give "structure" to spontaneity, by consciously going against the grain in order to generate an outcome that is surprising to everyone else, but not to you (there is a summary in the Appendix). This is similar to the *think, do* principle we looked at in the last chapter. The lesson is: work out what to do and then do it. Or, as we said at the beginning of this chapter:

1. Know what you need to do.
2. Write a list.
3. Do it.

Views of the experts

There are two particularly good sources of advice when it comes to getting things done. In his book *Getting Things Done*, David Allen maintains that it is possible for a person to have an overwhelming number of things to do and still function productively with a clear head and a positive sense of relaxed control. He recommends that you should:

1. Have only one filing system.
2. Turn your in-tray upside down and work on the principle of First In First Out (FIFO), not LIFO (Last In First Out) as many people do.
3. Have a five-stage system: collect, process, organize, review, do.
4. Do it, delegate it, or defer it.
5. Spend no more than two minutes on anything.
6. Never put anything back into your in-tray.
7. Concentrate on the very next physical action required to move the situation forward.

The more relaxed you are, he claims, the more effective you will be (as in karate). Applied to all parts of your life, and not necessarily the most urgent bits, this becomes Black Belt Management.

In *Simply Brilliant*, Fergus O'Connell quite rightly points out that the best ideas aren't always complicated and the incredibly straightforward stuff is often overlooked in the search for a complex answer. He proposes seven principles that can be adapted for attacking most everyday problems:

1. Many things are simple – despite our tendency to complicate them.
2. You need to know what you're trying to do – *many don't*.

3. There is always a sequence of events – *make the journey in your head.*
4. Things don't get done if people don't do them – *strategic wafflers beware.*
5. Things rarely turn out as expected – *so plan for the unexpected.*
6. Things either are or they aren't – *don't fudge things.*
7. Look at things from other's point of view – *it will help your expectations.*

In a world of over-complication, asking some simple questions can really make your life easier. For example:

• What would be the simplest thing to do here?
• Describing an issue or a solution in less than 25 words.
• Telling it as though you were telling a six-year-old.
• Asking whether there is a simpler way.

Both books are summarized in the Appendix.

Tick Achieve as a way of life

Once you have mastered some of these new approaches, and found them to be working well, you need to set about making them habitual. They need to become a way of life. We will look at this in detail in Chapter 7. In the short-term, there are only two questions that can truthfully establish if you are making any progress:

1. So have you done it?
2. No really, have you?

They appear to say the same thing, and in a sense they do. There is, however, a good reason for this. Extraordinarily, some people have developed the ability to say they have done something when really they haven't. How is this possible? It all seems to revolve around whether a task is started or finished. To be clear about this:

Just because a task is started doesn't mean it is finished.

The only definition that matters when it comes to *Tick Achieve* is:

A task is only finished when it is finished.

It is between the starting and the finishing that people manage to convince themselves that the job is done, when actually it isn't. So, returning to the question: *So have you done it?* If the task is started, but not finished, then the answer is no. If it is finished, then the answer is yes. That's why the fail-safe *No really, have you?* plays such an important double check.

> *"I find that the harder I work, the more luck I seem to have."*
>
> **Thomas Jefferson, quoted in The O'Reilly Radar**

How to *Tick Achieve*

To summarize what we have covered in this chapter:

- To tick off is to move on – get into the habit of starting tasks, finishing them, and ticking them off.
- You need some structure otherwise you will be approaching tasks in a random way.
- Try to adopt the idea of a boxy mind – think of it as a phrenologist's head with different tasks in different compartments.

- Concentrate on the skill of great list writing – don't live with the poorly written scraps of paper that you currently have.
- Consider the different sets of criteria in the PERFECT system – if one set doesn't do the job, then compare two types.
- Distinguish between the Vital, Preferable and the Nice to have.
- If you prefer a visual approach, then use the Priority Matrix.
- Develop the knack of spotting bad lists and don't accept them.
- Don't talk too much about it: do it.
- Trust your instinct when deciding what course of action to take.
- Try to turn *Tick Achieve* into a way of life.
- Just because a task is started, it doesn't mean it is finished – a task is only finished when it is finished.

Look Lively

6

"I may look inert but my brain is doing a one hour cardio workout."

This chapter covers how liveliness of the mind is more effective than any physical activity. The rigour of vigour; the more you do, the more you will get done. Energy and the art of effective activity. Getting your attitude right and how to Walk TALL. Conquering the quotidian and liberating more time for the things that you find enjoyable. The joys of experimentation. Laziness versus liveliness, and when to do nothing. The value of self-editing and why quantity is no substitute for clarity. Outline of how to look lively.

Liveliness of the mind is more effective than any physical activity.

The rigour of vigour

We have come a long way since the first chapter. We have investigated how businesses often fail to demonstrate the kind of intelligence that would enable them to get things done more effectively, how talking straight and leaving things out clarifies tasks so much more easily, how celebrating small victories helps forward motion, and how to develop a system for tackling multifarious tasks. That's good progress and, in a sense, we could stop right there. If you believe that you now have all the necessary skills to *Tick Achieve*, then I would strongly suggest that you just get on with it.

There are, however, a few tonal issues around the whole subject of getting things done that are worth chewing over – the sorts of nuances that could help the advanced *Tick Achiever*. So in the second half of the book we are going to look at the levels of energy that are desirable to get lots of things done, how to "outthink" yourself by facing up to your failings, and how to be encouraged by progress rather than constantly striving for elusive perfection. Finally, we will summarize how all this can be applied to businesses, and to you, the individual.

The first area is that of energy. As you can see from the quote at the beginning of this chapter, I believe that liveliness of the mind is more effective than any physical activity. This does not mean that I think people should remain static all day dreaming up world-beating ideas. Physical movement in the broadest sense is good too. My point is that far too much physical energy is expended on initiating and completing tasks that have no essential purpose. It is always better to think first, then act second. So let's concentrate on how lively mental energy translates into appropriate physical action.

Look lively:
1. Hurry up
2. Get busy

Both definitions of the title of this chapter have merit. *Hurry up* applies to all those things that can be done without much thought because they are uncomplicated, undemanding or fundamentally routine. Get these small irritations out of the way as quickly as possible in any given hour, day, shift, week, month or year. *Get busy* has particular relevance to anybody who suffers from prevarication, procrastination or borderline indolence. There is no getting away from it:

The more you do, the more you will get done.

Getting busy, in the sense of being appropriately busy on a range of activities and getting them done effectively, is highly desirable. I am not proposing being busy for the sake of it, or creating the appearance of being busy, or doing lots of things without really knowing why. None of these displacement activities have any bearing whatsoever on your ability to *Tick Achieve.*

What we are celebrating in this chapter is the value of energy – in business, and in life generally. This is the spark that makes someone say: *"They're great – full of ideas and enthusiasm."* It's a brilliant quality and we should all aspire to it. Not only does it do wonders for other people's opinions of you, it also does wonders for you personally. The more you fizz, the better you feel. The better you feel, the more you get done. The more you get done, the more you fizz. And so on. I call it the rigour of vigour.

Energy and the art of effective activity

Energy:
1. Intensity or vitality of action or expression
2. Capacity or tendency for intense activity: vigour
3. Vigorous or intense action; exertion
4. The capacity of a body or system to do work

The Greeks had this down pat. Their word *energeia* meant activity, and *energos* means effective. Put it all together and the best definition you will find of energy is effective activity. Activity in its own right is irrelevant. If it is ineffective, then you might as well have not done anything at all. The effective element makes the whole thing worthwhile. That's why the basic equation we examined in Chapter 1 is so crucial: *"If I do x, then y will happen . . ."* To *Tick Achieve* successfully, it is essential to work out whether any action you take will be effective.

Looking at the modern definitions of energy, some elements are more desirable than others. Intensity or vitality of expression is to be valued so long as it manifests itself as enthusiasm and passion, rather than antagonism or confrontation. Intensity of action is good in the sense of short, sharp execution of a job that does not infringe on anybody else, but may be less appropriate where a task needs sensitive handling. A capacity or tendency for intense activity is good if you plough through mundane stuff in a brisk manner, but bad if you become too intense or stray into (over)exertion. One way or another you need to develop the capacity to do effective work whilst applying appropriate blasts of energy to the right things in the right areas. The fewer areas and the more effective the actions, the better your results will be.

> *"Rise early, work hard, strike oil."*
>
> **J. Paul Getty**

Getting your attitude right

Energy and vigour are closely linked to attitude. If your attitude isn't right, you will never get anything done successfully for yourself, let alone anyone else. Here is a five-point plan for ensuring that it is:

1. You need to be on the ball.
2. You need to be organized and efficient.
3. You need to understand the link between action and effect.
4. You need to understand the value of politeness.
5. You need to understand the crucial difference between service and being servile.

Being on the ball means staying abreast of developments, not being caught on the hop, thinking ahead and keeping an open mind. Organization and efficiency is what this book is all about. Action and effect is the *"If I do x, then y will happen . . ."* principle. Politeness has the power to buy you time and ease tricky situations. Providing excellent service can include recommending the opposite of what you have been asked to do. Servility is the automatic enacting of whatever you are told, which is frequently the opposite of what would be advisable.

Walk TALL

So we are on our way towards drawing up a blueprint for lively, energetic behaviour that forms the cornerstone of the effective completion of tasks. You will have come across expressions such as *"You get out what you put in"*, *"You reap what you sow"* and *"Do as you would be done by"*. The same principle holds true for the degree of energy you care to put into your completion of tasks. The more you do, the more you will get done. It's a chain reaction of sorts.

Lively:
1. Full of life or vigour
2. Vivacious or animated
3. Busy; eventful
4. Having a striking effect on the mind or sense
5. Refreshing
6. In a brisk manner

Look at these definitions of the word lively. It's a great list, isn't it? Who wouldn't want to have dinner with someone who was full of life and vigour, vivacious, animated and refreshing? They certainly would have a striking effect on your mind or senses. Undoubtedly the encounter would be busy and eventful, but also thoroughly rewarding. These are the sorts of qualities to which you should aspire, and it is energy that holds the key to liveliness, mental or physical. For those of you who like mnemonics, my little mantra for this is:

Walk TALL

TALL stands for *Tick Achieve* Look Lively. It works in both directions, so if you Look Lively you are more likely to *Tick Achieve*, and vice versa. It's a virtuous two-way equation.

Conquering the quotidian

One quite common reaction to the idea that people should be as lively as possible as often as possible is that it is easy to say but very difficult to do day in day out when things are actually quite repetitive. It's a fair point, and one that I will examine now. As a child in French lessons, I had to complete an exercise every day. They were called quotidians (literally "dailies"). Quotidian in English means recurring daily, or describes something that is everyday or commonplace. Conquering the quotidian is a crucial part of being able to *Tick Achieve* successfully, and there are various ways to do it.

Unless you are the world's luckiest person, there will be plenty of things that you have to do that you would rather not. That's life. Paying bills, doing chores, repetitive tasks – they all fall into the box of quotidian nausea. We can bellyache as much as we like but they still have to be done, and that fact is never going to change. So we may as well develop some decent coping strategies to ease the monotony. This is my four-point plan for doing just that:

1. Do the worst first.
2. Do the worst fast.
3. Complete the necessary quickly.
4. Liberate more time for the enjoyable.

Doing the worst first makes eminent sense. If you don't like doing something, then do it straightaway and get it over with. As we established in Chapter 3, tasks do not improve in quality if they are delayed.

Doing the worst fast is also highly advisable. Obviously if it is a time-consuming exercise, then there will be a limit to how fast it can be done. But do make sure that you push that limit. Spend as little time as possible doing things you don't enjoy and, if humanly possible, don't do them at all.

Completing the necessary quickly refers to doing the "must do" items as efficiently as possible. That doesn't mean shoddily or unprofessionally. It just means what it says: quickly. Do it in the Greek spirit of *effective activity* that we looked at earlier in the chapter.

So here comes the crucial bit. All the above means that you can:

Liberate more time for the things that you find enjoyable.

When it boils down to it, that's what this book is all about. There may be those who choose to interpret the spirit of *Tick Achieve* as a system for over-delivering, doing too much and generally being macho. But as I stated at the very beginning of the book, that's not what I have in mind. Life is complicated enough as it is. Let's use efficiency and an ability to *Tick Achieve* to facilitate a better quality of life.

The joys of experimentation

So let's assume that you have developed the knack of doing the worst first and fast, completing the necessary quickly, and so have freed up more time than usual for the things that you find enjoyable: now what? This is where we encounter the joys of experimentation.

> *"When you come to a fork in the road, take it."*
>
> **Yogi Berra**

The word experiment, disregarding for a moment meanings derived from the world of science, means:

1. An attempt at something new or different.
2. An effort to be original.

Both these meanings are rather brilliant. Doing something new or different is so fundamental to life that it can hardly be overstated. Variety is indeed the spice of life, and those who do very little or are too bound up in doing the irrelevant are missing out. They are unlikely to be fulfilled. By contrast, those who intentionally pursue something new or different are likely to enjoy the diversity. Making an effort to be original is equally valuable. What would life be like without all those great people who strive to invent new things? All of us can contribute, even if in small ways, and it should be our intention to do so as often as possible, whether in a work, personal or social context. All of which suggests the addition of a fifth point to our plan for conquering the quotidian:

1. Do the worst first.
2. Do the worst fast.
3. Complete the necessary quickly.
4. Liberate more time for the enjoyable.
5. Try anything once.[*]

> *"I'm always doing things I can't do, that's how I get to do them."*
>
> **Pablo Picasso**

Point number five causes consternation in certain circles. I am not suggesting a dash for hedonism, perversion or law-breaking. What I am proposing is the propagation of an inquiring mind and the energy and drive to get out and try new things. For a full analysis of this approach, have a look at my previous book, *So What?* Apart from the thrill of discovering new and interesting things, one of the greatest effects of having tried something is that you have actually done it. As such, you are then in a position to comment on it. Far too many people these days are quick to pass judgement on things of which they have no experience. To avoid doing this, try more. It will increase your experience and broaden your palette of opinion.

Laziness vs. liveliness

The alternative to an energetic approach is laziness. Idleness, indolence, call it what you will. Even the very words to describe it make you feel sluggish:

---

[*]So long as it is legal.

Lazy:
1. Not inclined to work or exertion
2. Conducive to or causing indolence
3. Moving in a languid or sluggish manner

In her controversial book *Hello Laziness*, Corinne Maier provides a counterpoint to all those who suggest that increasing productivity is the key to success. She says that you can be a slacker and get away with it, and that only by reducing your productivity to zero do you have any chance of climbing the corporate ladder. Hard work and long hours won't get you anywhere, she says. The backdrop to this book is corporate France, where civil servants have index-linked jobs for life and can barely be fired. No wonder, in a recent survey, 75% of all French teenagers aspired to be one. And yet behind the cynicism, there is an interesting point to be debated. A sensible amount of hard work probably will get you somewhere. What is pointless, however, is hard work and long hours for the sake of it. Your objective should be to do the minimum amount of *highly effective* work in order to liberate the maximum amount of time to do the things you treasure. I believe they call it work/life balance. (There is a summary in the Appendix.)

> *"Rest is a good thing, but boredom is its brother."*
>
> **Voltaire, quoted in The Times**

Do bear in mind, of course, that having free time all the time could be almost as bad as working 100% of the time. Pleasure is nothing without pain. Summer is nothing if you haven't lived through winter. It's the old yin and yang thing. So rest and leisure are good, so long as they provide a pleasant contrast to activity and work. As Voltaire points out, you don't want to stray into the realms of boredom.

A man who has an interesting take on this whole area is Ricardo Semler, a Brazilian who runs a massive set of companies and insists on working in an unconventional way. He likes to question everything, and in his book *The Seven-Day Weekend* he asks, among other things:

- Why are we able to answer emails on Sundays, but unable to go to the movies on Monday afternoons?
- Why do we think the opposite of work is leisure, when in fact it is idleness?
- Why doesn't money buy success if almost everyone measures their success in cash?

By all accounts, his company is an extraordinary place in which workers choose their bosses, financial information is shared with everyone, board meetings always have two vacancies for any members of staff who want to attend, and a high percentage of employees determine their own salaries. Among his ideas for maintaining staff loyalty and interest are:

- *Retire a little* (take Friday afternoons off and offset it against retirement age).
- *Up 'n Down Pay* (vary hours and pay to suit circumstances).
- *Work 'n Stop* (take long periods off but declare intention to return).

There is a summary of his philosophy in the Appendix. What is the relevance of all this? The lesson is that humans require and desire a sensible balance of work and play. Too much or too little of either leaves us frustrated. So to the over-workers: slow down and take a break. To the lazy ones: look lively – you'll enjoy it more.

For a complete rundown on the differences between work, hard work and clever work, when not to work hard, or at all, when laziness does work, understanding the link between effort and results, and why lazy people achieve nothing, have a look at my previous book *Start* (chapter 6).

When to do nothing

So somewhere between total laziness and relentless liveliness lies a happy balance. Those at the livelier end of the spectrum will of course get more done. There are, however, some circumstances in which it can be positively beneficial to do nothing at all. This is another piece of Ricardo Semler's reverse psychology. The reaction of most people when something unexpected or apparently detrimental happens is to take some remedial action. Perversely, he suggests that when anything untoward happens you should do nothing at all on the assumption that good sense will eventually sort it out. It's a sort of non-interventionist style that relies on the prevailing mood. If people are essentially grown-up, then eventually they will resolve things. So next time something goes wrong, consider doing nothing.

The value of self-editing

Another helpful skill to develop with regard to looking lively is the ability to self-edit. You will be familiar with people who talk too much. Because they pursue a "word dump" strategy, they fail to self-edit. In modern business, this problem also applies to written presentations. Most are far too long. In a recent project, I was asked to analyse the last six presentations made by a particular company trying to win new business. There were over 800 charts in total, the average number of charts was 84, and the longest contained 124. None of them had won the business. Although these figures sound colossal, I subsequently met a frustrated Regional Director who had just been sent a proposed presentation to a prospect that was 650 charts long. She was exasperated, and could not find a theme in it at all.

We established in Chapter 3 that brevity equals intelligence. If you want to keep your energy levels up and *Tick Achieve* more consistently, then you need to self-edit. It is your responsibility to spend a few minutes examining your line of thinking to work out if it is clear and appropriate. If it isn't, then change it. This will save hours of random debate with other people, many of whom will either not understand what you are going on about, or will merely conclude that you are a vague waffler. This approach applies equally to written work. There is a tendency in the modern business world to hide behind mountains of data, often completely unedited. This creates the impression of rigour where there is none, and offers a safety blanket for the under-confident manager. Be certain of one thing:

Quantity is no substitute for clarity.

So make sure that you can self-edit. It will improve your ability to communicate, increase your reputation as a clear thinker, and contribute to the maintenance of high energy levels. Above all, you will get a lot more done in far less time.

How to look lively

So let's wrap up what we have covered in this chapter:

- Liveliness of the mind is more effective than any physical activity – don't rush about for the sake of it. Deploy mental energy first, then apply an appropriate amount of physical energy on the most relevant action.

- The rigour of vigour will see you through the most demanding of situations – regard your energy as an important asset.
- The more you do, the more you will get done – although this sounds potentially tautologous, it really does work.
- Understand the difference between effective and ineffective activity – there is no point in vigorously applying the wrong action.
- Getting your attitude right will increase your chances of being able to *Tick Achieve*.
- Walk TALL (*Tick Achieve* Look Lively) is a little mantra that works in both directions: the more you get done, the more energy you will have, and vice versa.
- Conquering the quotidian (making light work of mundane tasks) is a crucial skill to develop – do the worst first and fast, and complete the necessary quickly.
- This will liberate more time for the things that you find enjoyable, which is the underlying principle of *Tick Achieve*.
- Constant experimentation will make your life richer.
- A healthy balance between laziness and liveliness is desirable, but it requires constant adjustment.
- There are times when it can be better to do nothing at all.
- Self-editing is an essential skill that you should work hard to adopt.
- Quantity is no substitute for clarity.

Outthink
Yourself

7

"Some of my best ideas were
from thinking inside the box"

This chapter covers why knowing what you are unlikely to do can increase your likelihood of doing it. The art of anticipation. The excuse culture: glossing, glazing and glozing. If you want to get something done, stick to the facts. How facing up to your failings allows you to get more done. The art of outthinking yourself. Finding your locus of control. Prearranging tripwires and fail-safes. Dealing with lateness, disorganization, doing everything at the last minute, forgetting things completely and being unable to remember names. How winning sportspeople have already pictured themselves winning. It's urgent (pretend it's not). It's not urgent (pretend it is). Ratiocination and the one thing intelligent people know. Outline of how to outthink yourself.

Knowing what you are unlikely to do can increase your likelihood of doing it.

The art of anticipation

So let's assume that you have a decent system and plenty of the right sort of energy. What else can possibly get in the way of your getting things done? One obvious answer is forgetfulness. This does not have to mean that you suffer from amnesia or any other memory-related difficulty. More likely, you just have a huge number of things to do. The more you need to do, the more likely you are to miss something. There will also be occasions when even your brilliantly constructed list won't help. That could be because you are not physically near the list, or you are moving so swiftly that you haven't looked at it recently. There is also the fraught area of knowing that, no matter how good your system is, your personality keeps trying to avoid doing things. In your struggle to tame your random side, there are lots of things you can do to outthink yourself. Whatever the reason, this chapter looks at clever little tricks you can play on yourself to increase the likelihood of getting something done.

The psychology behind this is that knowing what you are unlikely to do can increase your likelihood of doing it. Although this may sound contradictory, it isn't. Let me explain why. Millions of people fail to do things, and yet do nothing to change their behaviour. The simple process of recognizing that you may well fail to do something is the first stage in ensuring that you do it. It's a mini-admission of a failing, and once you have admitted it, you can set about working out how to rectify it.

This is the art of anticipation. In short, if you can anticipate what you will probably fail to do, you can devise clever ways of making sure that you don't fail.

> *"I get up every morning determined to both change the world and have one hell of a good time. Sometimes this makes planning my day difficult."*
>
> **E. B. White, quoted in The Sunday Times**

The excuse culture

We live in an excuse culture. People have always got a reason as to why they haven't done something helpful, or have done something unhelpful. This is all very well if people are trying to wriggle out of tight situations or avoid being fired, but it is a poor way to proceed with yourself. In other words, if you allow yourself to accept your own feeble excuses, then you are only deluding yourself. You mustn't let this happen if you genuinely want to *Tick Achieve*. This is not supposed to be a heavy subject, but it does involve a good degree of self-discipline. As an amusing interlude, here is my A–Z of why nobody ever says what they really mean these days.

Alcohol: *"I was drunk so either I didn't mean it or I can't remember what I said."*

Bullshit: *"I am talking in riddles to disguise the fact that I don't have an opinion."* (see Chapter 2)

Celebrity: *"I am terribly important, or at least I think I am."*

Drugs: *"My cocktail of uppers and downers has left me confused."*

Evasiveness: *"Like a politician, I am going to make it sound like I am giving an answer without actually doing so."*

Fear: *"I know what to say but am too scared to say it."*

Greed: *"I'm not going to say that because I will lose out."*

Hubris: *"I am too proud and arrogant to get involved in that."*

Ignorance: *"I genuinely don't know what to say or how to say it."*

Jargon: *"I am still talking in riddles."* (see B)

Knowledge: *"I have no idea."* (see I)

Laziness: *"I want the world on a plate."* (see Chapter 6)

Materialism: *"I only talk about things that make me money."*

Newspapers: *"I have read other people giving endless excuses so I am going to do it too."*

One-upmanship: *"I suffer from status anxiety and want to appear better than everyone else."*

Politics: *"I don't want to be associated with that or I don't want the blame if it goes wrong."*

Quacks: *"My therapist says I have X syndrome which explains why I never come to the point or get anything done."*

Religion: *"It's nothing to do with me. It's all down to a divine power."*

Sexuality: *"That's man's/woman's work."*

Television: *"I have seen people on the TV giving endless excuses so I am going to do it too."* (see N)

Understanding: *"I haven't paid enough attention so I don't understand what I am talking about."*

Vanity: *"This conversation is, quite frankly, beneath me."*

Workshyness: *"I am not saying a word otherwise I will be given more work to do."*

Xenophobia: *"I am so scared of strangers that I'm not saying a thing."*

Yellow streak: *"I am too cowardly to come to the point."*

Zodiac signs: *"My horoscope explains why I never say or do anything constructive."*

This could equally be an A–Z of Self-Deception. One way or another, it's a right royal list of why things are not going to get done. Have a quick look at the list. If you recognize yourself in any of the comments, ask yourself whether you are preventing yourself from getting things done. If so, try making some changes to your approach.

"Something must happen: that is the reason for most human relationships."

Albert Camus, quoted in The Independent

Glossing, glazing and glozing

Gloss over: to hide under a deceptively attractive surface

Glaze over: (of eyes) to become glassy

Gloze: to explain away

It's funny how all these words merge into one. Anyone who glosses over the truth is to be treated with suspicion. All the more daft if that person is you and you are simply deluding yourself. Those in the unfortunate position of having to listen to someone who is glossing over the facts may well find themselves glazing over. The mind wanders when things become vague because there is nothing for the brain to latch onto. Gloze is a seldom-used verb that means to explain away. As a noun, it means flattery, deceit, or deceptive talk or actions. So, glozing is to be avoided when you are trying to get things done. What it essentially boils down to is:

If you want to get something done, stick to the facts.

Facing up to your failings

If you want to outthink yourself, you first need to face up to your failings. The purpose of this is so that you can recognize what you tend not to do well, and then set about working out ways to work around these deficiencies. Mostly, these are just small shortcomings that are mildly irritating, but if you have several deficiencies they can put some fairly large barriers in the way of you completing tasks. Let's look at some examples:

- Do you have a tendency to be late?
- Are you fairly disorganized?
- Do you leave things to the last minute?
- Do you often forget things completely?
- Do you have trouble remembering names?

Knowing yourself helps to address these problems and get more done. Hopefully, you don't suffer from all of the above. If you do, then work on one issue at a time – don't try to fix everything at once.

Being aware of your failings allows you to get more done.

The art of outthinking yourself

Outthinking yourself requires that you use your calm, controlled moments in order to anticipate what you will get wrong or fail to do at a later uncontrolled moment. If you often forget your house keys, then put a note on the back of the door to remind yourself. If that doesn't work, then keep a spare set at work or with a neighbour. If you often run out of petrol, then put a note on your steering wheel saying petrol. If you always forget birthdays, then put them in your diary in big red pen with a reminder three days before, or set a reminder to check at the beginning of each month. The knack is to admit at the outset that you

---

"One person with belief is equal to a force of 99 who have only interests."

John Stuart Mill, quoted in The Economist

will probably not do the job, and then work out the most effective way to make sure that you do.

Your locus of control

Grabbing control of this whole area and taking responsibility for your actions is what psychologists call your locus of control. It was Julian Rotter who introduced this idea in 1947 as part of his Social Learning Theory. He believed that there are basically two types of people, depending on their upbringing. Those with an internal locus of control believe that reinforcement depends on personal efforts. They think they are in charge of their lives and act accordingly. They are physically and mentally healthier and more socially skilled. Their parents tend to have been supportive, generous with praise, consistent with discipline and non-authoritarian. Those with an external locus of control believe that reinforcement depends on outside sources – so they make less attempts to improve their lives and get things done. If you want to pursue this further, have a look at *Introducing Psychology* by Nigel Benson.

Clearly, you cannot change your upbringing, but you can aspire to the qualities represented by an internal locus of control. That means taking responsibility for your actions, recognizing that improvements can be made, and acknowledging that it is down to you. It's no good sitting passively claiming that there is nothing you can do, because

> *"You can say, 'Gee, your life must be pretty bleak if you don't think there's a purpose.' But I'm anticipating having a good lunch."*
>
> **Jim Watson, quoted in The God Delusion by Richard Dawkins**

there is, and that is what this book is all about. So what can you do exactly?

Prearranging tripwires and fail-safes

What you need to do is to set up tripwires and fail-safes that ensure you do get everything done at the right time. It takes a balanced mind to admit that things will go wrong before they do, but it isn't a complicated idea. If you can face up to it, then with a bit of forethought, it won't go wrong. So let's return to the examples we looked at just now. Here are the sorts of tripwires and fail-safes you can set up.

Lateness
- Set your alarm earlier.
- Set your watch ten minutes early as a permanent feature.
- Take a few minutes to look at your day, week or month and anticipate the tricky points.
- Calculate the travelling time to each of your destinations and be aware when to set off.
- Decline last-minute requests that will make you late.
- Plan your time assuming you will have interruptions.
- Pretend you have a hot date and you have to be on time.*

Disorganization
- Choose a system and stick to it.
- Review all the things you have missed out on by being disorganized.
- Review the effect your disorganization has on everyone else.

---

*This is what Fergus O'Connell calls – the *"hot date"* scenario.

- Try every trick this book suggests.
- Ask others to help you.

Everything last minute

- Review the financial cost of doing everything at the last minute.
- Review the emotional cost of doing everything at the last minute.
- Try doing something well in advance once, and see if you prefer the feeling.
- Choose someone you care about, and arrange something for them.

Forget things completely

- Write a list of the things you regularly forget.
- Invent a tripwire for each one and enact them immediately.
- Always build in extra time before the crucial moment or day to allow you to recover your position.

Can't remember names

- Pay careful attention when you are introduced to someone.
- Repeat their name out loud.
- If the name is unusual, ask how to spell it.
- Ask for surnames as well as first name or forename – they are often more memorable.
- On the way to an engagement, run through people's names if you can remember them, or ask a colleague or partner for reminders.
- If in a meeting, write them down straightaway.
- If it's a big meeting, ask for a list of attendees in advance and study it.
- If it's a conference, take the list of delegates with you and check it from time to time.

There are hundreds of little things you can do to make things better. If you make the effort, there are two superb effects:

1. You get more done, so you feel more fulfilled.
2. You get more done, so others appreciate you more.

That's a hell of a combination. Who wouldn't want to be more fulfilled and more appreciated?

Pretend the job is finished

This book would be bigger than the *Old English Dictionary* if it attempted to anticipate every tripwire that you might ever need. So instead take the spirit of these few examples and try to apply the principle behind them to your own life. If you like the idea of outthinking yourself, then here are three pieces of kidology that might help to kickstart your approach to getting things done:

1. Pretend the job is finished – how did you do it?
2. It's urgent – pretend it's not.
3. It's not urgent – pretend it is.

Pretending the job is finished is a non-scary way of envisaging the end result without actually doing anything. This enables you to work out how best to do it and whether it is worth doing. What does the end result look like? How many ways of achieving that are there? What is the easiest and most effective method? How long will it take? What are the different stages? This is a simple technique similar to that employed by winning sportspeople. Every time the gold medallists at any given competition are interviewed they say the same thing:

Winning sportspeople have already pictured themselves winning.

So if you really want to *Tick Achieve*, then picture yourself having already done it all, and then work backwards in your mind to work out how to get there.

It's urgent – pretend it's not

Trick number two is to take something that is genuinely urgent and pretend that it's not. What happens? You relax a bit, take the pressure off, and think more clearly. The extraordinary thing about thinking clearly is that it takes no longer than panicking. And yet the results are so much better. The precise timeframe of this approach is almost immaterial. If an immediate response is required (for example, a direct question from someone who is standing right in front of you), then two seconds may be all you need to provide a better answer or think of a better way forward. If it's an urgent recommendation for today, then five or ten minutes might do the trick.

> *"Treat all disasters as if they were trivialities but never treat a triviality as if it were a disaster."*
>
> **Quentin Crisp, quoted in Forbes magazine**

It's not urgent – pretend it is

Many people fail to get things done because they have convinced themselves that there is plenty of time. This approach rarely works well. In extreme cases it manifests itself in the Essay Crisis syndrome so beloved of students the world over. Amazingly, they claim to work better under pressure, which is patently nonsense. For a complete rundown on why essay crises don't work, have a look at my previous book, *So What?* Far more important than banishing non-urgent tasks to the back of your mind is the fact that you may well be able to solve them quickly anyway, if only you can be bothered to try it now. So if it isn't urgent, try pretending that it is. If something doesn't need doing for two weeks, pretend it is needed this afternoon. Your first reaction as to what will do the job has a very strong chance of being right and effective.

In his book *Blink*, Malcolm Gladwell says that our ability to "know" something in a split-second judgement, without really knowing why we know it, is one of the most powerful abilities we possess. A snap judgement made very quickly can actually be far more effective than one we make deliberately and cautiously. By blocking out what is irrelevant and focusing on narrow slices of experience, we can read seemingly complex situations in the blink of an eye.

This is essentially "thinking without thinking". He introduces the theory of "thin slicing" – using the first two seconds of any encounter to determine intuitively your response or the likely outcome, and he demonstrates that this "little bit of knowledge" can go a long way, and is accurate in over 80% of instances.

Recommending ratiocination

Ratiocinate: to think or argue logically and methodically; to reason

What it all boils down to is a concerted attempt to think logically and methodically. If that doesn't work, then try outthinking yourself. Either way, the endpoint will be the same – a greater frequency of being able to *Tick Achieve*. I recommend ratiocination and I am all in favour of outthinking yourself.

There is a direct link between these characteristics and psychological health. Abraham Maslow, the spiritual father of humanistic psychology, introduced his hierarchy of needs in 1970. It showed that self-actualization (realizing your full potential) can only be achieved if your other needs are essentially fulfilled. These are physiological, safety, love and belongingness, self-esteem, cognitive, aesthetic and finally self-actualization. He demonstrated that psychologically "healthy" people show very consistent characteristics:

1. An objective perception of reality.
2. Acceptance of their own nature.
3. A commitment and dedication to some type of work.
4. Naturalness, simplicity in behaviour and spontaneity.
5. Independence; a need for autonomy and privacy.
6. Intense mystical/peak experiences.
7. Empathy with, and affection for, all humanity – including strong social interests.
8. Resistance to conformity.
9. Democratic characteristics.
10. Keenness to be creative.

It's a wonderful list of attributes, and one to which we should all aspire. If you can manage to tick all the above, then you will undoubtedly be able to *Tick Achieve*.

The one thing intelligent people know

It's a funny thing, but you do hear it fairly often. Someone who doesn't value their own opinion much says to another:

"It's alright for you – you know everything", or *"You think you know it all"*. And yet if there is one thing that all intelligent people do know, it's that they have a lot to learn. That's why they are always learning new things – because they know it never ends and they find it fascinating on the way.

> *"Most scientists are bored by what they have already discovered."*
>
> **Matt Ridley, quoted in The God Delusion by Richard Dawkins**

So to be effective at getting things done you need to look relentlessly for new and interesting ways to keep yourself stimulated. Play tricks on yourself. Try to outthink yourself. View tasks and issues in different ways. Take a variety of views on time, pressure and workload. Push the variables around a bit. Enjoy the whole business of getting things done rather than seeing it as drudgery. As the old academic saying goes, there is no such thing as an uninteresting subject, just a disinterested student.

> *"Contrary to popular belief, my experience has shown me that the people who are exceptionally good in business aren't so because of what they know but because of their insatiable need to know more."*
>
> **Michael E. Gerber, The E Myth Revisited**

How to outthink yourself

To recap what we have covered in this chapter:

- Knowing what you are unlikely to do can increase your likelihood of doing it – start by recognizing this.

- It is important to develop the art of anticipation so that, within reason, you can predict what will fail to get done based on an honest understanding of your character.
- The excuse culture encourages people to get away with not doing things – don't fall for it.
- Glossing, glazing and glozing are all pointless activities that prevent you from getting things done.
- If you want to get something done, stick to the facts.
- Being aware of your failings allows you to get more done – face up to your failings and work out how to outthink yourself.
- Understand your locus of control and try to make it internal.
- Prearrange tripwires and fail-safes to tackle failings such as lateness, disorganization, doing everything at the last minute, forgetting things completely and failing to remember names.
- Winning sportspeople have already pictured themselves winning – try pretending that the job is finished and envisage how you got there.
- If it's urgent, pretend it's not.
- If it's not urgent, pretend it is.
- Ratiocination is desirable – try to think logically and methodically.
- The one thing intelligent people know is that they have a lot to learn – adopt the same inquisitive approach.

Progress Not Perfection

"We have an eight month log-jam, but we can add your project to it, no problem."

This chapter covers why the fact that nothing is perfect needn't stop you making progress. The difference between quantitative and qualitative perfection. Are you just doing it or doing it well? Go for progress not perfection. Apogees and brobdingnagian achievements. Moments of greatness and whether they are possible. Gaining control of yourself. Establishing your liminal limits and how to observe them. Dyspeptic diversions and why they don't help. Outline of how to make progress without perfection

The fact that nothing is perfect needn't stop you making progress.

There are two distinct schools of thought when it comes to the pursuit of perfection. Some believe it is crucial, others believe it is a waste of time or, at best, unachievable. I can see merit in both views, but for the purposes of those who wish to *Tick Achieve*, I fall in favour of progress over perfection. This chapter explains why.

The relevance of perfection depends tremendously on the context in which it is pursued. Those designing and manufacturing physical products that are related to life or death situations should certainly strive for perfection. This would include planes, trains, ships, cars, space rockets, ski lifts, hang gliders, and so on. They clearly need to strive for perfection but they don't necessarily achieve it as various accidents sadly demonstrate. Then there are those products which may well strive for perfection, but whose context could hardly be described as crucial. Luxury goods such as watches and pens spring to mind. Such objects begin to span the divide between function and form. At the other end of the spectrum, artists, poets and writers are often cited as striving for perfection, but the territory in which they operate is by its very nature opinion-based and, as such, qualitative. This is why we must distinguish between quantitative and qualitative perfection.

Quantitative and qualitative perfection

What this essentially means is that perfection is relative. I only half agree with the old adage that if a job is worth doing then it is worth doing well. Actually, it rather depends on what the job is. There are hundreds of tasks that need to be done but they do not need to be done well. Let's look at some examples:

- Paying the gas bill.
- Putting the laundry in the washing machine.
- Buying some stamps.

At basc level, these jobs cannot be done well or badly. It is only if you pay the gas bill late, put the washing on the wrong cycle or put the wrong stamps on a certain parcel that the task assumes a qualitative dimension. To clarify:

Quantitative: the job just needs doing, full stop. You can tick the jobs off numerically and view them as a quantity of things to be done.

Qualitative: the job needs doing well. The quality can be demonstrably better than if it is done badly, and high quality should be your goal.

There is a massive difference between the two. Take any of your lists and separate the tasks by those that simply need doing and those that need to be done well (that is to say, to a certain standard that is discernible by you or anyone else that matters). It is hard to generalize about this because it depends somewhat on how many functional tasks you typically have to do, but the percentage is likely to be high. Everything of this nature should be done as fast as possible, with no delay and without much thought. It's functional stuff. That leaves more time for those tasks that need more care and attention and, ultimately, more time for relaxation and recreation.

Just doing it or doing it well?

Even those tasks that require an element of quality do not necessarily require perfection, if indeed it can ever be achieved. There are many different scales of quality, for example:

• Awful
• Bad
• Poor
• Average
• Good
• Better
• Best
• Ultimate

The descriptors don't really matter. The point is that there is a scale that runs from not very good to superb. Everybody has their own standards. No one will admit to wanting something that is poor, bad or awful, and the same applies when you are trying to get things done, so we are going to ignore the substandard classifications for our purposes. All we require is a simple three-point scale of:

1. Average
2. Good
3. Brilliant

Now we are well on the road to being able to grade tasks by their likelihood of reaching the dream state of perfection. Take one of your task lists and attribute an A, G or B rating to each task (average, good or brilliant). The findings can be quite surprising. There are hundreds of routine things for which an average grade is quite sufficient. These are the jobs for which no qualitative measure is relevant. The fact is it doesn't matter how you do them, they just need doing. Equally, there are plenty of things where a good execution of the task is absolutely fine – you don't need to achieve top of the range for these either. Which leaves the items to which you have assigned a B. For these, do your very best.

Progress not perfection

Is your very best perfect? I doubt it. Mine never is. This is the dilemma with striving for perfection. There is nothing wrong with it as a life philosophy, but it simply cannot be applied to everything that needs to be done. There are two fundamental problems with perfection:

1. Perfection may not exist.
2. Perfection may never quite arrive.

Before you throw your arms up in protest and claim that I am advocating substandard work and aiming for underachievement, ponder this: how can anyone ever prove that something is perfect? My contention is that, precisely because perfection is a qualitative notion, it is unhelpful to pursue it for the purposes of getting things done.

This is a point that I outlined in a previous book, *Start* (chapter 2). Too many businesses sit around pontificating about the so-called "perfect" solution that is just around the corner. The trouble is, around the corner is where it usually stays. This is equally true of those wanting to *Tick Achieve*. If you genuinely think you can find perfection, then hats off to you. More often than not though, people will use the chimera of it as an excuse not to proceed. So aim for progress, not perfection. It will get you far further than the pursuit of some El Dorado that never arrives.

> *"If you want to succeed, double your failure rate."*
>
> **Thomas Watson, quoted in The Independent**
> **On Sunday**

People often fall into the trap of making a strange connection between success and perfection. And yet nothing could be more imperfect than those who achieve success. Their road to achievement is usually littered with false starts and mishaps. Successful products are preceded by many prototypes, many of them defective. The more mistakes you make, the more you learn. Even when successful people or companies reach the mythical "top" of their fields, there are always imperfections and their attendant surprises to come. Striving to do something better is admirable, but do bear in mind that perfection may be a mythical construct than can never be achieved.

Apogees and brobdingnagian achievements

So we have established that a crucial part of the *Tick Achiever*'s armoury is the ability to distinguish between those things that are worth trying to do well, and those that just need to be done, full stop. Without this ability, you are likely to suffer from three possible impediments:

1. Spending too much time on things that don't warrant it.
2. Spending too little time on things that do warrant it.
3. Becoming so muddled between the two that nothing gets done at all.

None of which need prevent you from having high standards. Quite the opposite, in fact. The very ability to distinguish between the different types of task should free you up to devote quality time to those things that merit detailed attention. Then you can aim for your apogee.

Apogee:
1. The point when the moon is furthest from the earth
2. The highest point

High points and immense achievements are all relative. If you achieve something that you have never done before, then that is a high water mark. This could be anything from passing a driving test to completing your first painting, cycling from London to Brighton or building a kitchen. It's all relative to the individual.

> *"Success is relative. It is what we can make of the mess we have made of things."*
>
> **T. S. Eliot, quoted in The Independent**

What feels small to one person may be brobdingnagian to another. Brobdingnag was a fictional land occupied by giants in Jonathan Swift's satirical novel *Gulliver's Travels*. Lemuel Gulliver visits it after the ship on which he is travelling is blown off course and he is separated from his party. He describes it as a continent-sized peninsula six thousand miles long and three thousand miles wide, with a range of volcanoes up to 30 miles high. Swift was highly sceptical about the reliability of travel writings and these unlikely geographic descriptions parody many unreliable travel books published at the time. The adjective brobdingnagian has since come to describe anything of colossal size. A brobdingnagian achievement would certainly be big.

But big doesn't necessarily mean good or desirable. Spend a little time determining what you deem to be an achievement and how large or small it needs to be to give you satisfaction. Sift the tasks that don't inspire you that much from those that do. By all means aim for that once-in-a-lifetime nirvana, but also keep an eye on the fictional El Dorado problem we looked at in Chapter 2 (*The fine art of business fiction*). If such a state of affairs can ever exist, it is likely to be elusive or at best fleeting. More likely, you will be capable of moments of greatness, and that's what we are going to look at now.

Moments of greatness

If you only ever did one great thing in your life, what would it be? How many times do you expect to hit the top? How often might you achieve peak performance? Will you ever? Being realistic about these goals is a crucial part of working out what you can get done and what may be too fanciful.

Robert Quinn, writing in the *Harvard Business Review*, suggests that even the most successful leaders in the world only ever have temporary *moments of greatness*. They are at the top of their game when they act from their deepest values and instincts. Usually they tap into these fundamental qualities during a crisis, but actually it is possible to do so at any time if you get in the right frame of mind. The literary world is full of books about leadership, each one typically proposing a magic formula whereby, if you follow the golden rules, you too can be a top-performing businessperson. But Quinn tries to demonstrate that when leaders do their best work, they don't copy anyone at all. They just draw on their fundamental instincts. You can do this too. Look at the differences in approach when you move from your normal state to the fundamental state he describes:

Normal state	Fundamental state
Stick with what I know	Venture beyond familiar territory to pursue ambitious new outcomes
Comply with others' wishes in an effort to keep the peace	Behave according to my values
Place my interests above those of the group	Put the collective good first
Block out external stimuli to stay on task or avoid risk	Learn from my environment and recognise when there's a need for change

The purpose of this analysis is not to stray into idealism or altruism. It is easy enough to translate this learning from the big corporate stage to the tough reality that we individuals face every day. If you want to *Tick Achieve* more effectively, you can increase your chances by:

1. Being true to your principles.
2. Recognizing when change is needed.
3. Learning to do different things.
4. Learning from external stimuli.

The last two seem the same but they are not. Learning to do different things is practical, whereas learning from external stimuli is experiential. In his extraordinary book *An Intimate History of Humanity*, Theodore Zeldin shows that the essence of mankind is based on curiosity. Without it, we often fail to see the point of living. So if this lies at the very heart of our character, why would we not wish to pursue it with gusto? Given that so many parts of our lives revolve around getting things done, why not apply the same appetite for learning to achieving that aim?

> *"Failure is not falling down. Failure is falling down and not getting up again to continue with life's race."*
>
> **Richard Nixon, quoted in The Mail on Sunday**

Gaining control of yourself

The elusive quality of "being in control" has vexed people for years. As long ago as 1973, Alan Lakein (often described as a long-standing guru of time management) wrote a book called *How To Get Control Of Your Time And Your Life*. "Time is life", he asserted and promptly set about producing a system by which people could skilfully select the foremost tasks in order to (a) accomplish them and (b) do so in the best possible way. His main concept was controlling time, and he believed that this must be done with balance – neither too tight nor too loose. According to him, three groups of people misuse time management principles and lose control. They are:

1. **The over-organized** person who is more interested in *feeling* organized than in actually accomplishing anything.
2. **The over-doer** who is always busy doing things, but seldom takes the time to assess the value of what she is doing. As a result, she only gets a lot of low-priority projects completed.*
3. **The "time nut"** who is so preoccupied with time that he never wastes a second. He knows how to get everything done a couple of seconds quicker.

---

* *In this politically correct age, I should point out that the choice of a female here is Lakein's, not mine.*

All three types of people drive everyone around them completely nuts. The point is that life is a never-ending stream of possible activities, constantly being replenished by your family, your teachers, your boss, your subordinates, as well as by your own dreams, hopes and desires, and by the need to stay alive and functioning. You cannot carry out goals – you can only carry out activities. That is why you need to *Tick Achieve* each day. Among his suggestions for getting things done, Lakein offers some wonderful nuggets of philosophy:

- Perfection is a waste of time when completing low-priority tasks.
- Accept the fact that, at your choosing, some tasks are better left undone.
- Find prime times during the day when you characteristically do your best work, and plan your time blocks accordingly.
- Arrange for quiet times, breaks from extended activities, and times to simply do nothing.
- Balance work and play – you will get more done in the long run.
- Train yourself to use your subconscious during your sleep to help you solve difficult problems.*
- Wean yourself off television.
- Do your best and consider it a success.

These pieces of advice are timeless, and I couldn't put it better. Ten years later, Dru Scott put an eighties (and female) perspective on the whole issue with her book *How To Put More Time In Your Life*. She found that, even though she was teaching and writing about time management, she was

---

* *This is similar to the "Trust your* Depth Mind" *concept that we investigated in Chapter 3.*

always rushing from one appointment to another. After finally admitting that she was failing to keep her own counsel, she came up with the following three-step plan.

1. **Clarify priorities:** concentrate on quality activities; fulfil your wants as well as your objectives; define and do what really counts.
2. **Understand what motivates you:** face up to mixed feelings in yourself and others; reward and reinforce the best in yourself and others; motivate yourself every day to do what's important.
3. **Do your best with this day:** don't wait to live fully; open yourself to the joys of the moment; go ahead, do it – the best time is now.

> *"Success is going from failure to failure without loss of enthusiasm."*
>
> **Winston Churchill, quoted in**
> **The Sunday Telegraph**

It is not a coincidence that Scott has a list of irritating Compulsive Controllers similar to that of Lakein. Here are her five types of what these days would be called control freaks.

1. **Hurry up:** puts things off until the last minute and then is forced to rush.
2. **Be perfect:** wastes time on trivial, peripheral matters.
3. **Please me:** yearns to satisfy everyone, and often over-commits.
4. **Try hard:** wants to be recognized for trying hard, even if failure is the end result.
5. **Be strong:** doesn't believe in asking anyone for help and must continually declare independence to prove self-worth.

Do you recognize yourself in any of these types?

What's happening?

In his book *Why Entrepreneurs Should Eat Bananas*, Simon Tupman suggests a number of ways of working smarter not harder. Many people assume that if they work harder they will earn the freedom they desire. Yet working hard and being busy does not achieve this. This is a slave strategy. The smarter ones have some or all of these traits:

• They are recognized as an expert at something.
• They work more on their business than in it.
• They have a sense of purpose.
• They strive to be excellent in all they do.
• They leave customers better off than when they met them.
• They learn to say no.
• They are action-oriented.
• They stay in great SHAPE.*

We have touched on many of these points in previous chapters but, as ever, let's try to strip it down even further to things that you can apply right now in even the most basic of circumstances. If you want to *Tick Achieve*, try this simple four-part system for classifying the things you have to do:

1. Happening.
2. Not happening.
3. On hold for the moment.
4. Recycle for later.

* *Skills, Health, Attitude, Persistence, Enthusiasm.*

This can be applied to a day, week, month or year. Let's assume that you are looking at what to do today. Go to your list and identify everything that needs to happen today (type 1). These tasks come top and must be done today. Strip out anything that, on reflection, doesn't have to be done (type 2). Consign these to the bin and never do them. It just isn't worth it. If you are uncertain about how to classify a task, then it is probably a type 3 or 4. These involve two slightly different reasons for not doing something today. Type 3 means that you are putting something on hold for a moment because it is not as urgent as a type 1. The length of the hold needs to be established and you need a system to make sure that you revisit them at the right time. Type 4, recycling for later, applies to things that you suspect will be relevant one day, but their immediate need is not apparent. Use this classification for materials and ideas that could come in handy one day but whose need isn't evident right now.

Liminal limits

The spirit of *Tick Achieve* is to get the job done so that you can have more time to enjoy yourself and improve the quality of your life. Remember that Alan Lakein states that perfection is a waste of time when completing low-priority tasks, and Dru Scott's "Be perfect" type of control freak wastes time on trivial, peripheral matters. It is essential therefore that you develop the ability to distinguish between hardcore tasks and peripheral froufrou. I call this defining your liminal limits.

Liminal: Relating to the point (or threshold) beyond which a sensation becomes too faint to be experienced

---

This is an adjective often used by psychologists to describe the outermost reaches of consciousness and experience. If you visualize your set of tasks as an overhead view of a fried egg, then you need to concentrate on the yolk in the middle. From time to time you may need or wish to do things in the white area. But never do things beyond the limit of the egg. Should you choose to do so, you will fall into the trap defined by Lakein and Scott, and will waste your time. This may well irritate you, and you can be sure that it will aggravate those around you. If the task in question is too faint to make a difference, then don't do it. Recognize your liminal limits, and don't go beyond them.

Dyspeptic diversions

One final word on the whole business of pursuing perfection. For many, it makes them very grumpy. Dyspeptic is a wonderful adjective, derived from the stomach disorder dyspepsia. Dyspeptic people are irritable, which is no fun for them or anyone who comes into contact with them. It is possible to get a lot done when you are a curmudgeon, but it is equally likely that you will achieve much less than someone who approaches their tasks with a positive attitude and a decent sense of humour. Grumpiness is essentially a diversion. It distracts you from getting things done, so try to avoid it as much as you can.

> *"Some folk want their luck buttered."*
>
> **Thomas Hardy, quoted in The Independent**

The world does not organize itself to suit your every need, although the way some people behave, they clearly think that it should. As we mentioned at the beginning of this chapter, the fact that nothing is perfect needn't stop you making excellent progress. Have a careful think about what "perfection" means to you, and whether it is actually more realistic to aim at doing functional things in a functional way, and more important tasks well. See if you can grab a moment of greatness here and there. Understand your limits and enjoy working with them. Go for progress, not perfection.

> *"If at first you don't succeed, failure may be your style."*
>
> **Quentin Crisp, quoted in The Independent**

How to make progress without perfection

So to summarize the main points in this chapter:

- The fact that nothing is perfect needn't stop you making progress. Be realistic about your targets and set them at appropriate levels for the nature of any given task.
- Quantitative and qualitative "perfection" are quite different things. If you can measure your definition of perfection, then define it and go for it. If not, be careful about how you define qualitative perfection – it may be too abstract to articulate clearly, so you'll never actually know if you have achieved it.
- Are you just doing it or doing it well? If it's a highly functional task, then average will do.
- You may be able to achieve moments of greatness. Analyse how well you perform in exceptional circumstances and try to harness those qualities in your everyday life.
- Gain control of yourself by applying a balanced view of *Tick Achieve*. Look at the irritating characteristics of

control freaks and try to eliminate them from your own approach.

- Try using simple systems such as *Happening/Not happening/On hold/Recycle* to clarify your daily tasks.
- Understand your liminal limits and don't go beyond them – it won't get you anywhere.
- Try to avoid dyspeptic diversions – you will suffer more than anyone, although it will also annoy everyone else.
- Go for progress not perfection.

Making Business Tick

"It wasn't a spectacular year but June was quite interesting".

This chapter covers how businesses can Tick Achieve, *and how most organizations are not well organized. Panjandrums and pirates. The year that never is. Why no company workforce ever works effectively for twelve months of the year. A new manifesto for business. Decision windows: are you deciding or just talking? Crisis Bombs and how to predict them. Monkey-free leisure time. Useless brainstorms and the cult of the manager. How to make business tick.*

Tick Achieve for businesses

So far we have mainly been discussing how to *Tick Achieve* in a personal context. In many respects, that's all that matters. However, it is worth spending a bit of time looking at how successfully (or unsuccessfully) organizations manage to *Tick Achieve*. They are, of course, made up of individuals, but much has been written about how individuals take on peculiar mass characteristics when they are assembled together. Take a look at what Mark Earls has to say in *Herd* (subtitled *How to change mass behaviour by harnessing our true nature*). There is a summary in the Appendix. It's a tricky business.

> *"Men go mad in herds, while they only recover their senses slowly, and one by one."*
>
> **Charles Mackay, quoted on openDemocracy.net**

What this essentially means is that even the most organized and reasonable people can act strangely when they work for an organization. Being well organized yourself is enough of a challenge for some people, and possibly the reason why you bought this book. Can you imagine then transferring that challenge to 10 of your staff? Or 100, 1000, or 100,000? This is the extraordinary task facing those running businesses. Just having a few staff involves tricky issues.

So this chapter takes all the ideas we have been looking at so far and tries to apply them specifically to businesses, or at least in a business context. All of us come into contact with organizations in one way or another. You may well work for one. Or with one, in a partnership. Or have one as a customer. Or simply be on the receiving end of their service. Of course it is easy to criticize, but you only need a couple of conversations in the pub to conclude that:

Most organizations are not well organized.

This assertion is not just a piece of random mud-slinging. Thousands of books have been written about how companies continually vacillate between not having enough staff and having too many. The never-ending cycle of hire and fire is as fickle as boom and bust in the financial markets. No one ever seems to learn, and it all happens again a few years later. Which begs the question: When, ever, do companies have the balance right? The work of Phil Rosenzweig's *The Halo Effect*, which we looked at in Chapter 2, suggests that it doesn't happen very often. Success, or the ability to *Tick Achieve* successfully, is fleeting for most corporations. Let's start to unpick why this might be.

Panjandrums and pirates

It is well known that many people overcomplicate things to make themselves appear more valuable. This deliberate obfuscation allows them to feel important, surround themselves in impenetrable jargon that needs unpicking, and charge more to those who don't know what they are talking about. Everyone has witnessed this behaviour in individuals at one time or another. There is no reason to assume, therefore, that this type will change at all when people gather together and represent a company. If left to their own devices, one would reasonably expect the number of obfuscators in any given corporation to mirror the percentage in the nation as whole. And yet something extra seems to happen in corporations. The percentage of this type of person seems to rise. Why is this? Process. Procedure. Company policy. Corporate culture. You can call it what you like, but some companies actively encourage their people to behave this way. They think it is for the common good, but the net effect is that everything slows down. Here are some examples:

Paralysis by analysis: *"I just need to crunch the numbers again."*
Bottlenecks: *"I need to run it by Geoff and he's away till next week."*
Fear: *"Heaven knows what Chicago will think of this."*
Prevarication: *"I think we'll put this on the backburner till Quarter 3."*
Indecision: *"I think we should let the market decide."*

Much of this stuff is perpetrated by the *Offlish* speakers we encountered in Chapter 2. Many are panjandrums. Panjandrum is the wonderful word for pompous self-important officials derived from a character call the *Grand Panjandrum* in a nonsense work by Samuel Foote, an English playwright and actor, in 1755. So what can a company do if it becomes apparent that many of these types are working for them, thereby inhibiting their collective ability to *Tick Achieve?*

> *"Whenever feasible, pick your team on character, not skill. You can teach skills, you can't teach character."*
>
> **Sir Ranulph Fiennes, quoted in The Sunday Telegraph**

There are two decent methods. The first is to hire for character, not skills. The second is to reward the *Pirates Inside* (I'll explain this in a moment). Look at the quote from Sir Ranulph Fiennes, a man who has been to the ends of the earth in genuinely extraordinary circumstances. When he is up against the toughest conditions that the world can throw at a person, he wants people with character. Of course his team need to know what they are doing, but without character, their ability to cope is diminished. Some more enlightened companies are only just beginning to realize this. For years they have been issuing briefs to head-hunters narrow-mindedly insisting on limiting criteria such as "relevant category experience essential", "market knowledge vital" and "minimum of three years in telecoms". This flies in the face of common sense and begs the time-honoured question: How does the man who drives the snowplough get to work in the morning? The amusing thing about it is that these requests presuppose that the markets are difficult to learn, which they usually are not. In other words, the writer of the brief for a new candidate is simply glorifying themselves and the supposedly complex nature of their work – a clear case of panjandrumic behaviour if ever there was one. Bright new companies recruit for character first, then teach the candidate the specific skills.

In *The Pirate Inside*, Adam Morgan argues that powerful brands are built by people, not by proprietary methodologies. The real issue is not the strategy, but how people need to *behave* when an organization's systems seem more geared to slowing and diluting than spurring and galvanizing. To achieve this they need to be Constructive Pirates. This is not the same as anarchy where there are "no rules", but it requires a different set of rules. You can spot these pirates by observing some of their ways of behaving. These include:

Outlooking: looking for different kinds of insights.
Pushing: pushing ideas well beyond the norm.
Wrapping: communicating less conventionally with customers.
Denting: telling it straight whilst still respecting colleagues.
Refusing: having the passion to say no.
Taking it personally: showing a different professionalism that transcends corporate man.

All of these qualities have merit when it comes to helping you *Tick Achieve*. We have talked about the importance of external stimuli – looking elsewhere for different ideas. Pushing beyond the norm, being able to say no, and telling it straight – a company must be able to do this if it is to get things done. There is a summary of the book in the Appendix.

The year that never is

No matter how much the people in a company attempt to *Tick Achieve*, there is always one thing that ruins it all: the forecast. I call it the year that never is. Never in the history of commerce has the forecast ever been the same as reality, and yet every year companies repeat the same forecasting mistakes. How every company gets it wrong, every year, is what we are going to look at next, because it is a crucial factor in explaining why they have trouble achieving what they want. The simple reason for this is that:

No company workforce ever works effectively for twelve months of the year.

Nevertheless the annual forecast, flying in the face of all common sense, blindly assumes that it does. In truth, most companies only work effectively for about five months of any given year. Take a look at Figure 9.1. They are below par for most of January, June, July, August and December, when half the staff are on holiday or in the pub. In February and September they are playing catch up. Which leaves March, April, September, October and November to get anything done.

THE PRODUCTIVITY CRISIS

Productive: 4 months (growth or recovery)
Underproductive: 5 months (stasis or decline)
Talking & Deciding: 3 months of decision windows (D) M/M/S
Crisis bombs*:   J/A/S

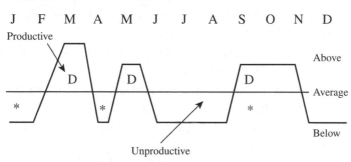

Figure 9.1   The productivity crisis

For those of you who feel that this is an exaggeration, take the summer of 2006 as an example. The United Kingdom effectively did no work at all during the (football) World Cup, and this is probably true of many nations. Then there was a heat wave, which ruled out any serious exertion in July. And with increasing Europeanization, almost nothing happens in August at all.

Finance Directors all over the world seem to completely ignore this phenomenon and thus totally miss the point when making their forecasts. Every year they use false metrics to convince the business (and themselves) that everything will proceed in an orderly fashion, which, of course, it never does. They persist in planning a twelve-month year, when no such working reality exists. No company is effective all the time, and their slavish adherence to planning a twelve-month year leads every year to the same thing – disappointment and frequently failure.

A new manifesto for business

If companies want to *Tick Achieve* more effectively, then they need to divide their time up much more realistically. A short ten-point manifesto for achieving this is:

1. Smaller chunks mean greater clarity – don't be seduced by massive plans.
2. Long-term plans are usually nonsense – resist them and don't believe them.
3. Decision windows are very short – use them wisely and rapidly.
4. There is a difference between talking and deciding – don't confuse the two.
5. Crisis bombs can usually be predicted – face up to it and plan for them.
6. Simplify things – don't overcomplicate them.
7. Monkey-free leisure time – work diligently, early on.
8. Eliminate useless brainstorms – let the ideas people generate the ideas.
9. Reduce the number of meetings – most are boring and a waste of time.
10. Eliminate the cult of the manager – they create the illusion of activity whilst not actually getting much done.

> *"Any idiot can face a crisis. It is day-to-day living that wears you out."*
>
> **Anton Chekhov, quoted in Time Out**

Let's work through the ten points in quick succession.

1. Smaller chunks

If the business that you work in or on is experiencing difficulties in getting things done, then try breaking everything down into smaller chunks. Greater clarity will emerge immediately. Start with straightforward questions such as: What action will be most effective here? What can we do *today* that will make a difference? Can I make that happen this week without fail? A corollary of this is that it doesn't pay to be seduced by massive plans. They may well be grandiose, but will they be effective? Too many executives have gone along with a grand scheme when secretly they believe it has no chance of happening.

2. Long-term fiction

The further in the future the predictions lie, the less accurate they are likely to be. And of course, a prediction is all that a forecast is. There's nothing wrong with sketching out guesstimates, but don't fall into the trap of believing that they are accurate. Every year in companies, beleaguered executives are asked to produce their best guess for the forecast. A few months in, they are being harassed by the Finance Director for not delivering the figures they offered up.

These long-term forecasts have a habit of turning into long-term fiction, so do your best to resist them in the first place, and don't trust them.

3. Decision windows

Have a look at Figure 9.1 again. The three peaks above the average productivity line are where all the decisions get taken. I call these decision windows. This is where the correct executives are all in the building at the same time (a very rare occurrence in modern business) and, crucially, they must all be in the right mood to make those decisions. This is usually when they are under extreme pressure and either undergoing, or envisaging, a crisis (see item 5). As you can see, the decision windows don't occur very often and the seasons are very short. By my calculation, they only constitute about three months of the year. That means the company can only generate forward motion in about 25% of its working year. If this is a problem that afflicts your business, I can offer two suggestions:

1. Make every effort to increase the length of the decision windows in your company.
2. Accept that the decision windows are very short, and use them wisely and rapidly.

4. Are you deciding or just talking?

Decision windows are short enough as it is, but there is another problem that often afflicts businesses: they often think that they are deciding when really they are just talking. There is a huge difference between talking and deciding, and if you want the business to *Tick Achieve* it is vital not to confuse the two. Many cultures (corporate or country) value talk more than action. We witnessed the culture of waffle in Chapter 2, and established in Chapter 5 that talk can be the enemy of action. As a national trait, that may not matter, but in business you cannot expect swift action if the culture is really just based around chewing the cud all day. If this applies to your business, do not be lured into believing that, just because people are meeting and talking, they are being decisive. It may not be true.

5. Crisis Bombs and how to predict them

Another feature of Figure 9.1 are the small asterisks, which designate Crisis Bombs. These occur because time has been squeezed into smaller pockets than the forecast suggested.

In essence, everyone agreed with the forecast because they thought that the company could achieve these targets in twelve months, which, if the workforce were fully operative for that period of time, it probably could. But because that is a falsehood, the year is squashed like a concertina. This causes Crisis Bombs to go off, usually about three times a year. Everyone has taken their eye off the ball for so long during the slack months that they panic and initiate poorly conceived ideas at very short notice. The irony is that Crisis Bombs can usually be predicted. Just take a piece of paper and sketch out the periods when it always goes wrong, face up to it and plan for them.

6. Simplify everything

Simplify things – don't overcomplicate them. Always ask yourself what the simplest thing to do is. If your business makes this more complex than it is, then try to change it. There are some excellent books that can help, such as *Simply Brilliant* by Fergus O'Connell and *The Laws Of Simplicity* by John Maeda. My own effort, *So What?*, also begs businesses to cut the fluff and get to the point in an effort to make everybody happier – by deploying the simple lines of enquiry adopted by children. Don't let anybody tell you that simple means simplistic – it might just be the best way.

7. Monkey-free leisure time

Have a look at Figure 9.2. This is a development of a theory I put forward in *So What?* (chapter 5). The *Considered* approach is propagated by wise cultures or individuals who "panic early" (or not at all) when approaching a deadline. They get the work done well before it is needed, and have the luxury of refining the quality of their output. More common is the *Essay Crisis* approach, reminiscent of students the world over, where everything is left to the last minute. When they arrive in the workplace, it is odd that so

DEALING WITH DEADLINES

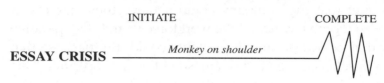

Figure 9.2   Dealing with deadlines

many graduates have failed to learn from the experience. They simply carry the practice into their adult life. Despite the plaintive cries of those who maintain that they work better under pressure, the truth is that, for the entire time that the work is not yet done, they have a monkey on their shoulder – maybe even several. This is the irritating voice in their head reminding them that they still haven't done the task. If people worked more sensibly and in good time, they would be able to enjoy *Monkey-Free Leisure Time*. If your business is a victim of this problem, then change it to work diligently early on, and then relax without that dreaded monkey.

8. Useless brainstorms

There is a common saying in this politically correct business world of ours: there's no such thing as a bad idea. Well actually, yes there is. A lot of ideas are absolutely dreadful, and not a second should be wasted considering them. Not only that, but a lot of time is spent in generating them, even though they have no useful value. The main culprit here is the dreaded brainstorm meeting. These are usually convened in a panic and almost every element of them is wrong: duration, venue and, astonishingly, the guests. How many times have people been told that they "must invite Geoff from production so that they buy into the whole process"? The fact is, Geoff has never had an original idea in his life, and he never will. Even worse, he may think he does and there is nothing more dangerous than an idea when it is the only one you have. At the end of the session, what have you got? Lots of random thoughts from a ragbag of people, and an action list that rarely gets done. So if you really want your business to *Tick Achieve,* let the ideas people generate the ideas, and eliminate useless brainstorms in favour of getting things done.

> *"The difference between creativity and innovation is the difference between thinking about getting things done in the world and getting things done."*
>
> **Michael E. Gerber, in The E Myth Revisited**

9. Meetings: who needs them?

Many meetings are boring and unproductive. They take too long and involve too many people holding court. In total, they take up far too much of the working week and prevent the attendees from getting on with the stuff that really needs doing. If this is a problem in your company, try some of these ideas:

- Only allow one topic per meeting – then discuss it in depth.
- Only allow ten minutes per item, which must be concluded by agreed action. This is the opposite of the previous idea, allowing many topics to be covered but in a strictly compact way, and always linked to action.
- Every meeting, introduce a perspective from a category that is completely different from the usual one.
- Every meeting, have a section on general business that is nothing specifically to do with the usual subject matter.
- Introduce a "No attendance, no role in the decision making" rule.

- Every attendee has to present an initiative, otherwise they can't come.
- Issue and rotate roles. At each meeting, a different person is in charge of time keeping, taking the minutes, chairing the meeting, confirming who is taking action, administering sanctions from the previous meeting, and so on. Everyone has to have a role.
- Introduce role-play exercises.
- Everybody has to fire themselves and walk back in with no preconceptions.
- Assume you are a new market entrant with little or no budget – what are you going to do?
- Introduce the ultimate sacrifice: What are we going to sacrifice to do one thing properly this year? Then, either do not meet for a year, or only meet to discuss the one thing.
- Ask the attendees what *they* want to discuss and get out of the meeting. The attendees can't complain about the agenda if they have written it themselves. If they refuse to contribute, then they should forego the right to have a bearing on decisions.
- Change the scenery to somewhere more distinctive – a castle, a church, a barn, or someone's house. This will create variety, make it more enticing to come, and should not necessarily be any more expensive than a hotel.
- Call in a facilitator, guest speaker, or even a comedian to break the pattern.
- Set activities during the meeting, rather than having presenters and an audience. They can be any blend of serious or fun.
- No one leaves the meeting until they have taken responsibility to do something. The whole exercise is reframed as action-orientated, and all information is disseminated outside of the meeting via intranet, so that the meeting never has the objective of conveying information.

- Introduce awards and penalties for action not carried out since the last meeting.
- Take the completely radical view that the meeting should be disbanded because it is not achieving anything.
- Write the minutes of the meeting before it takes place. This will ensure that you achieve what you need to.

10. The cult of the manager

One final point: the business world is now full of managers, and arguably too many of them. After all, if everybody is managing everyone else, then who is actually doing the work? Somebody has to, and that means having more doers than talkers. So if your company has wholehcartedly embraced the cult of the manager and created lots of layers that slow things down, then get rid of them. They often create the illusion of activity whilst not actually getting anything done.

> *"In the struggle between yourself and the world, back the world."*
>
> **Franz Kafka, quoted in The Sunday Telegraph**

How to make business tick

And so to summarize how you can apply the principles of *Tick Achieve* in a business context:

- Most organizations are not well organized – admit it and look for better ways to behave.
- Panjandrums will waste everybody's time and prevent things from getting done – instead hire and work with pirates who shake people up and get things done.

- The year that the forecast predicts never is – try starting a year without deluding everybody for once.
- No company workforce ever works effectively for twelve months of the year – stop calling it a twelve-month year and work out when the work really gets done.
- Smaller chunks mean greater clarity – break tasks down into sections and don't be seduced by massive plans.
- Long-term plans are usually inaccurate – resist the temptation to write them and if they do exist, don't believe they will actually happen.
- Decision windows are very short – recognize when they occur in your business and use them wisely and rapidly.
- There is a huge difference between talking and deciding – don't confuse the two or fall into the trap of believing that your business is getting things done when in fact people are just talking.
- Crisis bombs can usually be predicted – face up to the fact that they exist and plan for them.
- Simplify everything – this point does not have to be made more complicated.
- Monkey-free leisure time is available to everybody – work diligently early on and avoid essay crises.
- Eliminate useless brainstorms – there is such a thing as a bad idea and sometimes their effects can be disastrous, so leave it to the ideas people to generate the ideas.
- Reduce the number of meetings in your business – if yours are boring and a waste of time, try to shake up their format.
- Eliminate the cult of the manager – they create the illusion of activity whilst not actually getting much done, which will impede your company's ability to *Tick Achieve.*

Make Yourself Tick

10

"I've built a thriving business empire out of nothing but Dad's money and WEEKS of hard work"

This final chapter covers the complete Tick Achieve *method. What makes you tick? Why it is your responsibility to get things done – not someone else's. Monkey on your shoulder? Efficiency is a sophisticated form of laziness. In search of unworried Completer Finishers. How many hours in your life? The one-page personal plan. How to plan your year and improve your ticker. Three final critical questions and how to make yourself tick.*

The complete *Tick Achieve* method

We are approaching the end of our journey. For those of you who have read the whole book from beginning to end: thanks, and well done. Received wisdom has it that most people only read the first one or two chapters of business books. It is fascinating to draw together all the strands of why people struggle to get things done, how it can be made easier, and what the benefits are. You'll have realized by now that I am not remotely interested in getting more things done just so that you can do more things. Rather, completing necessary tasks rapidly and efficiently is a way to increase your peace of mind and leisure time. That's the benefit. If you succeed in applying the principles and techniques in this book, you should become much more efficient. If that is the case, then do make sure that you don't fall into the trap of accepting more tasks and creating more work for yourself. Resist this at all costs. Instead, use the time you have created to relax or pursue the things that interest you. You will be healthier, more contented and will probably live longer.

For those naughty readers who skip large chunks or just go straight to the last chapter to see what the whole point was, here is a quick summary of what *Tick Achieve* is all about. (If you want more detail, the numbers refer to their respective chapters.)

1. Business intelligence?

Business intelligence may well be an oxymoron. Many businesses do not always conduct themselves in a very intelligent way. Many businesspeople actually want to waste time because they are getting paid regardless of what they achieve. This is the opposite of how individuals and self-employed people behave – they just want to get things done so they can relax. Conversely, some people are addicted to work. They are incapable of switching off, and have lost sight of when a task is really finished, or when it could be. Others think that because a job is under-way, it is done, which it usually isn't. Many people have lost the ability to determine cause and effect: *"If I do x, then y will happen . . . "* And finally, much of what is done has no bearing on the main point – far too often, activity is confused with genuine action.

2. Thinking and talking straight

People who are incapable of coming to the point are, lit-erally, pointless. We live in a new world of waffle where nobody seems to talk straight. The problem is that if no one is talking straight then it is very hard for anyone to think straight. This degree of verbal nonsense has per-meated almost every walk of modern life, and in many businesses it is even actively encouraged. Ironically, therefore, the more incomprehensible a strategy, mission statement or presentation, the better it is perceived to be. This trend will take us all to hell in a handcart unless someone starts talking sense soon. Let that person be you. Learn to spot jargon and waffle for what it is, and work hard to avoid speaking it yourself. If you are truly duty-bound to speak like this at work, then either resign from your job or refuse to do so at home. A reasonable rule of thumb is that if you can explain something to your mother, then it is probably comprehensible and appropriately phrased.

3. Leave it out

Brevity holds the key to intelligence. The more you are able to eliminate, the faster you will reach sensible conclusions and get the right things done. Many thoughtful lines of inquiry will reveal that a lot of things actually do not need to be done at all, thereby saving you hours of toil. Reductionism (in a practical rather than a purely philosophical sense) involves thinking harder and simplifying everything. Leaving it out, or considering doing so, forces the issue wonderfully. Try to adopt a boxy mind that categorizes what needs to be done. Write out anti lists of things that do *not* need to be done, or that you will never do. Tasks do not improve in quality if they are delayed, so do them now. Say no more often, adopt a system that suits you, and use it to your advantage. Once you have written something down then you can forget about it, but do also trust your *Depth Mind* (subconscious) to sort out difficult issues overnight. Less really is more.

4. One in a row

Achievement does not have to be a relentless series of successes, despite what many rather macho advisers might claim. Break big problems down into mini steps. You can eat an elephant if you take it a bit at a time. Rapid Sequential Tasking is just as effective at multitasking, so do things fast and one after the other if that way suits you better. Do not let technology hide the fact that you are disorganized. Never touch a piece of paper or email more than once. Think hard, then either do it, or don't. Keep an eye on how modern machinery causes attention deficit syndrome. If you want to get something done, turn off your mobile or hand-held device – you must rule them, not the other way round. Celebrate each small piece of progress and regard it as one in a row.

5. *Tick Achieve*

To tick something off is to move on – this bookends the fact that the job is done. You need some sort of system or structure to get a lot done. Some lists are next to useless, so you need to perfect the art of great list writing. There is a PERFECT system that might help you: Personal priority, Emotional importance, Reason for doing, Financial value to you, Everyone else's priorities, Chronological sift, and Time shifts. Experiment with how these help and choose a combination that suits you best. Talk can be the enemy of action, so don't confuse chatting about something with progressing. Instinct is a powerful thing – use it to spur yourself into action. Just because a task is started does not mean it is finished – it is only finished when it is finished.

6. Look lively

Liveliness of the mind is more effective than physical activity. Think hard and early, thereby preventing yourself from rushing about doing ill-judged things. The rigour of vigour suggests that the more you do, the more you will get done. It is important to get your attitude right and find ways to conquer the quotidian – mundane daily tasks that are not very exciting. Looking lively will liberate more time for the things that you find enjoyable. Be alert to external stimuli and try experimenting with new approaches. Liven up as many aspects of your day as possible – you'll enjoy yourself so much more. Develop the knack of being able to do nothing – either because it won't get you anywhere in a particular context, or because you have earned the rest. Quantity is no substitute for clarity. Understand and nurture the ability to self-edit.

7. Outthink yourself

Knowing what you are unlikely to do can increase your likelihood of doing it. The knack is to acknowledge your failings and put things in place to combat them. The modern excuse culture is a major culprit here – there always seems to be a reason why something hasn't been done. Unfortunately, the ultimate loser is always you, so don't demean yourself by allowing excuses to get in the way. Glossing over things doesn't work either, so if you want to get something done, stick to the facts. Establish your locus of control and prearrange tripwires and fail-safes to force yourself to do things. Persistent failings such as lateness, disorganization, forgetfulness and doing everything at the last minute can be rectified by using the *Tick Achieve* method. It's urgent – pretend it's not. It's not urgent – pretend it is. Winning sportspeople have already pictured themselves winning – picture the job finished and consider how you feel and how you did it.

8. Progress not perfection

The fact that nothing is perfect needn't stop you making progress. There is a huge difference between quantitative and qualitative perfection. Many tasks are mundane and cannot be done well or badly – they just need to be done. There is no point in wasting time on trying to do these quantitative tasks well because they cannot be done well. Average and fast will do fine for these. If a task can be done to a better quality standard, then by all means try to do it well. But aim for progress, not perfection. Perfection is an unquantifiable dream state usually reserved for artists and writers. Strive instead for brief moments of greatness, or an all-round better-than-average performance. Understand your liminal limits, beyond which it is unrealistic and unproductive to go. Avoid grumpiness and dyspepsia, and use a healthy dose of realism to add humour to even the most dreary of tasks.

9. Making business tick

Most organizations are not well organized. They try to make it look as though they are, but they're not. Some executives even thrive on disorganization, whilst simultaneously claiming not to like it. Many are full of panjandrums –

self-important and officious people who hide behind rank and process to slow everything down. What thriving companies need are pirates on the inside – people who don't mind cutting through the static to get things done. The annual forecast never is. No company workforce ever works effectively for twelve months of the year, and yet every year the Finance Director produces a work of fiction about what the business is apparently going to achieve (it rarely does). A new manifesto for business includes: being happy with smaller chunks; being wary of, or even ignoring, long-term fiction; recognizing that decision windows are short and infrequent, so use them wisely and rapidly; identifying the difference between deciding and just talking; predicting when Crisis Bombs will go off; simplifying everything; engineering *Monkey-Free Leisure Time;* cutting out useless brainstorms; reducing the number and nature of meetings; and cutting out the cult of the manager.

10. Make yourself tick
Part 10 is what this chapter is all about. We will draw together all the strands of the book and finish by asking you to look to yourself for the ultimate inspiration. After all, no matter how many writers offer their advice, and no matter how many books you read or how much experience you gain, it still falls to you to spring into action. My fervent hope is that there is plenty here to inspire you to *Tick Achieve*, but it's your call. Let's have a look at who you are.

What makes you tick?

Everyone has a different psychological profile and no book can generalize so much as to apply to everyone. Have a careful think about your personal style and cherry-pick the techniques that seem to work best for your character. It's very much a case of horses for courses. Pay particular attention to your failings – not to depress yourself, but so that you can recognize them for what they are; set up the necessary tripwires and fail-safes. Remember the excuse culture we looked at in Chapter 7? Don't become part of it. You need to identify the things that really motivate you, and try to spend as much time as possible doing those things, rather than the things you like less. In other words, the faster you complete the so-called nasty stuff, the quicker you can move on to nicer stuff. Above all though, bear in mind this crucial piece of information:

It is your responsibility to get things done – not someone else's.

When it boils down to it, it's your responsibility to get things done. Don't moan about it, and don't deny it. If the task is for you, then you will benefit. If the task is for someone else, then make sure you know why you are doing it and what purpose the completion of it will serve. If you don't know, ask. If you don't agree that it is worth doing, then consider not doing it. For more on how to deal with situations like this, have a look at my previous book – *So What?*

Monkey on your shoulder?

Have another look at Figure 9.2. Do you feel as though you have a monkey on your shoulder most of the time? Or several? When it comes to you personally, as opposed to your business or family, you owe it to yourself to reduce your worry levels as much as possible. You need to spend time working out how to engineer as much monkey-free leisure time as you can. As we saw in Chapter 6, the principle of *Tick Achieve* is to liberate more time for the things that you find enjoyable. It's not as difficult as it sounds. A simple checklist for doing so is:

1. Survey and organize all your tasks.
2. Do the simple, quantitative things as soon as possible.
3. Plan the high-quality tasks.
4. Don't leave things to the last minute.
5. Trust your instincts more and get on with it.

Efficiency is a sophisticated form of laziness

I was delighted to discover the following quote recently:

> *"One lets things descend into chaos because one can't be bothered to clean up, but then wastes hours trying to find socks or the right knife because everything is everywhere. Paradoxically, to be truly idle, you also have to be efficient."*
>
> **Tom Hodgkinson, How To Be Idle**

This is what I have been espousing for years. It's not so much the call to be organized that matters – it's what being organized can liberate on your behalf, and here is the confirmation. Even the most dedicated idler knows that efficiency is the springboard for idling. Now I am not suggesting that you use all your spare time for idling – that's your call. What I am asking is that you acknowledge the link between getting things done efficiently and your ability to have more choice, freedom and flexibility to do more of what you want. If you work for yourself, you might want to look at another of my books, *Start* (chapter 6).

In search of unworried Completer Finishers

In Chapter 4 we looked at the sorts of character traits that you need to develop in order to become truly successful at getting things done. We examined the Belbin system and identified the qualities that can help you to *Tick Achieve* effectively. These were:

Delivers on time
Imaginative
Reliable
Efficient
Conscientious
Turns ideas into practical actions
Solves difficult problems

In essence, this is the profile of an unworried Completer Finisher. Belbin highlights that Completer Finishers are wonderfully conscientious, but can also be anxious, inclined to worry unduly and are often reluctant to delegate. If we could take the worry element out of that description, then we pretty much have the perfect profile for someone who is going to *Tick Achieve*. So set your sights on becoming an unworried Completer Finisher.

> *"Only those who will risk going too far can possibly find out how far one can go."*
>
> **T. S. Eliot, quoted in The Mail on Sunday**

How many hours in your life?

If you live for 80 years (which of course you may not), then you will be around for about 645,000 hours. A third of this you will spend asleep, depending on your somnolent habits, so that reduces it to about 400,000 hours of waking time. For the purposes of *Tick Achieve*, it seems reasonable to remove childhood and school years, and everything post-retirement, which reduces the figure further to less than 200,000 hours. When you strip it down, you will spend around 80–100,000 of these working and 40–50,000 at leisure. Which begs the question: What will you be doing with this time?

There's nothing wrong with working for the man, so long as you have worked out why. There's nothing wrong with having lots of time off either, but use your time wisely. Remember, the more you get done, the more you can do.

The one-page personal plan

In my book *Start* I introduced the one-page personal plan. Here it is again in Figure 10.1. While you might feel a bit self-conscious doing such an exercise, I commend it to you as a good way of working out whether you are making

---

I stand for . . .

I am at my best when . . .

In five years I would like to be . . .

My ultimate dream is . . .

I will never . . .

I am going to start doing . . .

I am going to stop doing . . .

I will continue doing . . .

Figure 10.1 The one-page personal plan

good use of the time you have. We want to know what you stand for, when you are at your best, and what you would like to be doing in five years' time. The answers also allow you to work out what you *don't* want to do, and establish some plans for the future. All you have to do is complete the sentences.

If you can see a clear way forward, then you are well on the way to being a good *Tick Achiever*. But if you have no idea what you will be doing in five years' time, or you have no ultimate dream, then it may be time to take stock. There is no point in getting a lot done when you are heading nowhere, or if you are doing nothing whatsoever with the time that you are freeing up. You don't have to fill your days wall to wall, but it does pay to have a rough idea of where you are heading and what you want to do with those precious hours.

Planning your year

The same applies to the year ahead. Figure 9.1 showed that the year never happens in the way that is predicted. There are an infinite number of ways to fill out a calendar, so you might as well do it in a way that suits your style. If you work for a company, then there will be limitations, but if you work for yourself, then there won't. Design the year as you want it rather than letting events overtake you. Scribble down the months of the year and block out what you regard as a reasonable amount of work. Equally, score through those precious leisure times. Longer breaks are more productive than short ones. Try planning one. They deliver three times over because:

1. They take longer to plan, which gives you an exciting run-up.

2. They last longer, so the displacement from routine is more powerful.
3. The memories are more enduring.

Plan one of these annually and the interest should sustain you for the whole year. This principle also applies to months and weeks. Try to break up relentless runs of work, otherwise you will exhaust yourself.

Improve your ticker

Taking a sensible amount of time away from the grind of work is likely to reduce stress and lengthen your life. So does staying fit and healthy. Make sure that you don't misinterpret the *Tick Achieve* method as a call to get things done all the time, non-stop. This is almost the opposite of my message. The idea is to get all the necessary things done so you can either relax or do other things that matter to you. Of course, being healthy helps if you want to follow some of the advice in this book, particularly when it comes to looking lively. You need a reasonable amount of energy, both mental and physical, to *Tick Achieve*. But it's not supposed to be a relentless slog. The rewards are wonderful, but if you find the whole thing overwhelming, then stop. You'll know what your limits are.

> *"If you can't do it, give up."*
>
> **Sigmund Freud, quoted in The Times**

Three final critical questions

We're nearly done. I hope you have found some useful things here to help you *Tick Achieve*. No one can remember the contents of a whole book, so do dip back in from time to time. If you want to carry just a few thoughts around in your head, I would go for these three questions:

1. Do I really need to do this?
2. If I do x, what will happen?
3. If I don't do it now, when will I?

The first should always be your first port of call. If you don't really need to do something, then don't do it. The exceptions are of course gestures that are not essential but that add to the happiness of you or someone else. The second forces you to establish likely cause and effect. Knowing the likely outcome of an action is crucial in deciding whether to do it or not. And the third attends to the vexed issue of time. For all the great prevaricators amongst you, it's time to get on with it.

> *"You spend your life climbing up a slope and when you get to the top you get depressed because you've seen the end."*
>
> **Schopenhauer, quoted in The Sunday Telegraph**

How to make yourself tick

So to recap the main points of this last chapter:

- *Tick Achieve* means questioning business intelligence, talking straight, leaving many things out, celebrating one in a row, having a good system, writing good lists, looking lively, outthinking yourself and going for progress not perfection.
- It is important to ask yourself what makes you tick, and cherry-pick the elements of the system that suit you best.
- Do not spend your life blaming others or looking to them to realize your ambitions – it is your responsibility to get things done, not someone else's.

- If you spend a lot of time feeling that you have a monkey on your shoulder, then think more carefully about when you complete tasks so that you generate more monkey-free leisure time.
- Efficiency is a sophisticated form of laziness – use your newfound *Tick Achieve* skills to do less and free up more time.
- Unworried Completer Finishers deliver on time, turn ideas into practical action, solve difficult problems, are imaginative, reliable, efficient and conscientious – this is how you should try to be.
- Consider how many hours you will have in your life and don't waste precious time doing things you don't like.
- Fill in the one-page personal plan to articulate your goals.
- Plan your year, month or week – don't let them dictate to you.
- Improve your ticker – stay healthy and fit so that you have the energy to enjoy time on your own terms.
- If you remember nothing else from this book, try to memorize these three critical questions and use them to protect you from pointless tasks:
  1. Do I really need to do this?
  2. If I do x, what will happen?
  3. If I don't do it now, when will I?

Well, that's all from me. Now that I have finished writing this book, I can take some of my own advice, lean back, smile and say *Tick Achieve*.

"Happy endings depend entirely on stopping the story before it's over."

Orson Welles, quoted in The Sunday Telegraph

Bibliography

An Intimate History of Humanity, Theodore Zeldin (Vintage, 1998)

Blink, Malcolm Gladwell (Allen Lane, 2005)

Dangerous Company, James O'Shea & Charles Madigan (Nicholas Brealey, 2002)

Getting Things Done, David Allen (Piatkus, 2001)

Hello Laziness, Corinne Maier (Orion, 2005)

Herd, Mark Earls (John Wiley, 2007)

High Impact Speeches, Richard Heller (Pearson, 2003)

How To Be Idle, Tom Hodgkinson (Penguin, 2004)

How To Get Control Of Your Time And Your Life, Alan Lakein (Wyden, 1973)

How To Put More Time In Your Life, Dru Scott (Signet, 1981)

How To Tame Technology, Kevin Duncan (Hodder, 2013)

Introducing Psychology, Nigel Benson (Icon, 2004)

Liar's Paradise, Graham Edmonds (Southbank, 2006)

Moments of Greatness, Robert E. Quinn (Harvard Business Review, 2005)

Perfect Pitch, Jon Steel (John Wiley, 2007)

Revolution, Kevin Duncan (Hodder, 2011)

Run Your Own Business, Kevin Duncan (Hodder, 2010)

Screw it, let's do it, Richard Branson (Virgin, 2006)

See, Feel, Think, Do, Milligan & Smith (Marshall Cavendish, 2006)

Simply Brilliant, Fergus O'Connell (Prentice Hall, 2001)

Small Business Survival, Kevin Duncan (Hodder, 2010)

So What?, Kevin Duncan (Capstone, 2007)

Start, Kevin Duncan (Capstone, 2008)

Sun Tzu: The Art Of War For Executives, Donald Krause (Nicholas Brealey, 1995)

The Art of Creative Thinking, John Adair (Kogan Page, 2007)

The A–Z of Offlish, Carl Newbrook (Short Books 2005)

The Diagrams Book, Kevin Duncan (LID, 2013)

The Dictionary Of Business Bullshit, Kevin Duncan (LID, 2013)

The E Myth Revisited, Michael E. Gerber (Harper Collins, 1995)

The Halo Effect, Phil Rosenzweig (Free Press, 2007)

The Laws Of Simplicity, John Maeda (MIT Press, 2006)

The Pirate Inside, Adam Morgan (John Wiley, 2004)

The Seven-Day Weekend, Ricardo Semler (Century, 2003)

The Third Wave, Alvin Toffler (William Morrow, 1980)

Why Entrepreneurs Should Eat Bananas, Simon Tupman (Cyan, 2006)

Appendix

BOOK: *Blink*
AUTHOR: Malcolm Gladwell

What the book says

- Our ability to "know" something in a split-second judgement, without really knowing why we know, is one of the most powerful abilities we possess.
- A snap judgement made very quickly can actually be far more effective than one we make deliberately and cautiously.
- By blocking out what is irrelevant and focusing on narrow slices of experience, we can read seemingly complex situations in the blink of an eye.
- This is essentially "thinking without thinking".
- He introduces the theory of "thin slicing" – using the first two seconds of any encounter to determine intuitively your response or the likely outcome.
- He demonstrates that this "little bit of knowledge" can go a long way, and is accurate in over 80% of instances.

What's good about it

- There are scores of vivid examples in which people's first instincts have been right, but they cannot explain why. These include an art dealer identifying a fake statue that the Getty museum believes to be genuine, a tennis coach being able to predict every time when players are about to serve a double fault, and a psychologist accurately guessing years in advance if married couples will stay together or not.

- The thinking is a welcome counterpoint to a world in which too much reliance on proof and data has replaced hunch and instinct.
- The value of spontaneity is highlighted by the example of a forces commander who comprehensively beats better-equipped opposition in a US military exercise because he consistently does the opposite of what the computers predict.
- He goes on to show that, strangely, it is possible to give "structure" to spontaneity, by consciously going against the grain in order to generate an outcome that is surprising to the other party, but not to you.

What you have to watch

- Although the subject matter is fascinating, there are so many experts interviewed that the average reader would not be able to enact any of the skills necessary to take advantage of the findings, other than the basic point that you should trust your first instincts more.

BOOK: *Dangerous Company*
AUTHOR: James O'Shea & Charles Madigan

What the book says

- Extreme caution is needed when dealing with management consultants.
- There is a lot of information about the workings of Andersen, Boston Consulting Group, Bain, McKinsey, Gemini and their clients.
- You can find their products in here too – BCG's matrix (Growth; fast/slow – Cash; high/low – fill in stars/dogs/cash cows/question marks), the balanced scorecard and Gemini's transformation or re-engineering concept.
- It warns against fuzzy concepts like "world class" which cannot be defined or measured, and creating a "consulting fantasyland" which sounds reassuring but doesn't actually get you anywhere.
- Just before he died, McKinsey confessed that making real decisions in business is a lot harder than getting paid to advise people what to do – sometimes it is fine to admit that you don't have all the answers.

What's good about it

- There are many parallels to be drawn between provider/customer relationships and those between companies and consultants. There is a checklist of how to deal with consultants, which could equally apply to clients dealing with agencies:
  - *Why are you doing this?*
  - *Do you need outsiders?*
  - *Who will work on the business?*
  - *What will it cost?*

- *Never give up control*
- *Don't be unhappy even for a day*
- *Beware of glib talkers with books*
- *Value your own employees*
- *Measure the process*
- *If it's not broken, don't try to fix it*
- Being aware of these theories will increase your strategic capability.
- Consultants are better than most at applying market learnings from one client to another, and at repackaging their skills many times over.

What you have to watch

- This is not a classic marketing textbook where you can grab a few diagrams and claim you have read it – you need to absorb it and use the examples.

BOOK: *Getting Things Done*
AUTHOR: David Allen

What the book says

- It is possible for a person to have an overwhelming number of things to do and still function productively with a clear head and a positive sense of relaxed control.
- You should only have one filing system.
- You should turn your in-tray upside down and work on the principle of First In First Out (FIFO), not LIFO as many people do.
- It's a five-stage system: collect, process, organize, review, do.
- Do it, delegate it, or defer it.
- Nothing should take more than two minutes, nor go back into your in-tray.
- The four crucial factors are context, time, energy and priority.
- There is a six-level model for reviewing your work, using an aerospace analogy: 50,000+ feet: life; 40,000 feet: three- to five-year vision; 30,000 feet: one- to two-year goals; 20,000 feet: areas of responsibility; 10,000 feet: current projects; runway: current actions.

What's good about it

- If you have problems being organized and getting things done, this book will sort you out.
- The more relaxed you are, the more effective you will be (as in karate). Applied to all parts of your life, and

not necessarily the most urgent bits, this becomes Black Belt Management.

- You have to concentrate on the very next physical action required to move the situation forward. There are lots of good quotes:
  - *"This constant preoccupation with all the things we have to do is the single largest consumer of time and energy."*
  - *"Blessed are the flexible, for they shall not be bent out of shape."*
  - *"Everything should be made as simple as possible, but not simpler."*
  - *"I am rather like a mosquito in a nudist camp. I know what I want to do, but I don't know where to begin."*
  - *"The middle of every project looks like a disaster."*
  - *"Talk does not cook rice."*
  - *"There are risks and costs to a program of action, but they are far less than the long-range costs of comfortable inaction."*

What you have to watch

- Nothing. This is an international bestseller and it works.

BOOK: *Hello Laziness*
AUTHOR: Corinne Maier

What the book says

- This is an unusual book that provides a counterpoint to all those that suggest increasing productivity is the key to success.
- It says that you can be a slacker and get away with it, and that only by reducing your productivity to zero do you have any chance of climbing the corporate ladder.
- Hard work and long hours won't get you anywhere.
- Companies don't care. They hate individuals who don't conform.
- They talk gibberish, use people as pawns, and move them around so no one can keep track.
- They have no ethics, no culture, and have mastered the art of appearing more intelligent than they actually are.

What's good about it

- It's good to take the opposite view from time to time, if only to test what you believe.
- There are typologies of idiots: Mr Average, The Hollow Man(ager), Consultants who con, Timewasters, Yes-Men and Nobodies.
- The idea that business is effectively doomed is an intriguing one.
- What is a job for? Many workers genuinely don't know what they are paid for, so why should they fear being lazy?
- The author's ten new commandments of work are:
  1. Salaried work is the new slavery.
  2. It's pointless trying to change the system.

3. The work you do is fundamentally pointless.
4. You'll be judged on your ability to conform, not your work.
5. Never accept positions of responsibility.
6. Seek out the most useless jobs.
7. Hide away and stay there.
8. Learn how to read the subtle cues that tell you who else has rumbled all this.
9. Temporary staff do all the work – treat them well.
10. Business ideology is no more "true" than communism.

What you have to watch

- It is translated from the French and reflects many of the strange working practices in corporate France.
- If you choose to enact a large proportion of this book, you may get fired.

BOOK: *Herd*
AUTHOR: **Mark Earls**

What the book says

- It is subtitled *"How to change mass behaviour by harnessing our true nature"*.
- The main point is that, whilst everyone else is banging on about individual choice and one-to-one marketing, in fact everybody just copies, or is influenced by, other people.
- As such, most attempts by marketers to alter mass behaviour fail because they are based on a false premise.
- This is why most government initiatives struggle to create real change, why so much marketing money fails to drive sales, why M&A programmes actually *reduce* shareholder value, and most internal change projects don't deliver any lasting transformation.

What's good about it

- It explains the "why" of our struggles to influence mass behaviour.
- Most of us in the West have misunderstood the mechanics ("the how") of mass behaviour because we have misplaced notions of what it means to be human.
- There is a huge range of diverse anecdotes and evidence – from Peter Kay and urinal etiquette to international rugby and the rise of the Arctic Monkeys – to show that we are, at heart, a "we" species, but one suffering from the "illusion of I".

- It challenges most standard conceptions about marketing and forces the reader to rethink the whole thing.
- The seven principles of Herd marketing are:
  1. Interaction (between people)
  2. Influence (of certain people)
  3. Us-Talk (the power of word of mouth)
  4. Just Believe (stand for something and stick to it)
  5. (Re-)Light the fire (overcoming cynicism by restating the original idea)
  6. Co-creativity (let others join in)
  7. Letting go (you never were in charge of your brand)

What you have to watch

- Nothing.

BOOK: *High Impact Speeches*
AUTHOR: **Richard Heller**

What the book says

- It tells you how to deal with the request to make a speech – whether to accept the invitation, what to research and how to get the response you want.
- The right structure and preparation are essential, as are researching your audience, several edits and proper rehearsal.
- If you want to speak well, you need to know how to write, and vice versa.
- There are three basic principles for good speech-making: speak the truth; listen for the truth; be true to yourself.

What's good about it

- The book contains lots of good advice, and if you are anxious about making a speech, it guides you through the whole process.
- It is full of good quotes, such as:
  - *"It is significant that dumb has come to mean not only silent but stupid."*
  - *"Don't be patronising."*
  - *"Take some trouble to choose an accurate title."*
  - *"All speeches are essentially the same in architecture."*
  - *"Some speeches do not peter out but simply drop dead."*
  - *"A speech is a very concentrated form of conversation."*

- *"Almost every great speech changes pace several times."*
- *"No one likes a guest who domineers or rants or shouts."*
- *"Using negative arguments makes you sound negative, which is perilously close to being unpleasant."*
- *"Killer facts can come as shots or salvoes."*
- *"Rehearsal is an endless process of discovery."*
- *"Judicious silence has a mesmeric effect on an audience."*

- There are summaries at the end of each chapter to enable you to short-circuit everything.
- Some extracts from great speeches are included.

What you have to watch

- You can't just suddenly become a great speaker so, although this book provides a framework, it is no substitute for having an idea and a point of view.

BOOK: *Liar's Paradise*
AUTHOR: Graham Edmonds

What the book says

- 80% of companies think that they are fraud-free, but a recent survey actually revealed fraud in 45% of them.
- There are seven degrees of deceit:
    1. **White lie:** told to make someone feel better or to avoid embarrassment.
    2. **Fib:** relatively insignificant, such as excuses and exaggerations.
    3. **Blatant:** whoppers used when covering up mistakes or apportioning blame.
    4. **Bullshit:** a mixture of those above combined with spin and bluff to give the best impression.
    5. **Political:** similar to bullshit but with much bigger scale and profile.
    6. **Criminal:** illegal acts from fraud to murder, and their subsequent denial.
    7. **Ultimate:** so large that it must be true. As Joseph Goebbels said: "If you tell a lie big enough and keep repeating it, people will eventually come to believe it."

What's good about it

- It confirms what we all suspect – that the workplace constantly bombards us with lies, fakery and spin.
- Case histories of Enron, Boo.com, the European Union and others provide the proof on a grand scale.
- Deconstructions of other levels of lying help the reader to navigate their way through the day-to-day types. You can then decide how to react.

- It has tips on how to suck up to the boss, pass the buck and endure meetings.
- Everybody should read the chapter on Lies and Leadership.

"The truth is more important than the facts."

Frank Lloyd Wright

"Those that think it is permissible to tell white lies soon grow colour blind."

Austin O'Malley

"Honesty may be the best policy, but it's important to remember that apparently, by elimination, dishonesty is the second-best policy."

George Carlin

What you have to watch

- The book essentially condemns most corporate cultures and so needs to be viewed lightly by those who have to work in them.
- There is a moral dilemma lurking within: do you tell the truth and get trod on, or join the liars?

BOOK: *Screw it, let's do it*
AUTHOR: **Richard Branson**

What the book says

- Simple truths in life, and the right attitude, can inspire and enable you to do practically anything.
- People will always try to talk you out of ideas and say, "It can't be done", but if you have faith in yourself, it almost always can.

What's good about it

- You can read it in a couple of hours.
- The author has made plenty of mistakes and taken a lot of risks, so this is not just a "plain sailing" manual.
- The main principles of just do it, have fun, be bold, challenge yourself and live the moment are all solid, inspirational stuff.
- There are also much softer elements such as value family and friends, have respect for people, and do some good for others.
- You can dip in anywhere and grab a motivational thought in ten seconds.
- Choose from:
  - *Believe it can be done*
  - *Never give up*
  - *Have faith in yourself*
  - *When it's not fun, move on*
  - *Have no regrets*
  - *Keep your word*
  - *Aim high*
  - *Try new things*

- *Love life and live it to the full*
- *Chase your dreams but live in the real world*
- *Face problems head on*
- *Money is for making the right things happen*
- *Make a difference and help others*

What you have to watch

- The book is not particularly well written (the author struggled with mild dyslexia at school), so this is more a stream of consciousness, or a selection of sound bites.
- It always seems easier for someone who has "done it" to reflect back on the hard times – but it is harder to apply that philosophy when you are actually struggling.

BOOK: *See, Feel, Think, Do*
AUTHOR: Andy Milligan & Shaun Smith

What the book says

- Instinct is much more powerful in business than over-reliance on research or data, which can only provide you with a rear-view mirror picture.
- Focus groups and MBA models are not as good as human instinct or a passion to make a difference.
- By watching and empathizing with real customers and how they act, we can evolve better ideas that solve their real needs.
- *See, Feel, Think, Do* sums up how these intuitive ideas come to fruition.
- Why? is a powerful question and is not asked often enough in business.

What's good about it

See: Experience it for yourself
What is the current customer experience like? What do they value (or not)?
Feel: Empathizing with your customers
How do I feel about the experience? How do customers and employees feel? What do they like/dislike?
Think: There is no such thing as a stupid idea
Why do we do it this way? How could it be better? Why can't we do it?
Do: Make it so
What changes are needed to people, processes and products? How do we get our people and customers excited about it?

- This is a perfectly sound method that you can apply to any business to see what needs to be changed.
- There are scores of case histories to show how it all works (or doesn't): Carphone Warehouse, Apple iPod, Sony, Heinz, Harley Davidson, First Direct, Barclays, Geek Squad, Cathay Pacific, TNT, and more.

What you have to watch

- The *Think* premise that there is no such thing as a bad idea isn't right. There are clearly lots of bad ideas around.
- Whilst the process provides a framework, it isn't that remarkable. Good business people should be doing this instinctively anyway.

BOOK: *Simply Brilliant*
AUTHOR: **Fergus O'Connell**

What the book says

- The best ideas aren't always complicated and the incredibly straightforward stuff is often overlooked in the search for a complex answer.
- Many smart people lack the set of essential skills which could roughly be described as "common sense".
- There are seven principles here that can be adapted for attacking most everyday problems:
  1. Many things are simple – *despite our tendency to complicate them.*
  2. You need to know what you're trying to do – *many don't.*
  3. There is always a sequence of events – *make the journey in your head.*
  4. Things don't get done if people don't do them – *strategic wafflers beware.*
  5. Things rarely turn out as expected – *so plan for the unexpected.*
  6. Things either are or they aren't – *don't fudge things.*
  7. Look at things from other's point of view – *it will help your expectations.*

What's good about it

- In a world of over-complication, asking some simple questions can really make your life easier. For example:
  - *What would be the simplest thing to do here?*
  - *Describing an issue or a solution in less than 25 words.*

- *Telling it as though you were telling a six-year-old.*
- *Asking whether there is a simpler way.*
- Try writing the minutes of a meeting before the meeting – then you'll know what you want to get out of it.
- It highlights the difference between duration and effort. *"How long will it take you to have a look at that?" "About an hour."* But when?
- It explains the reasons why things don't get done: confusion, over-commitment, inability – usually busy people never say there's a problem.
- Plan your time assuming you will have interruptions – the *"hot date"* scenario.

What you have to watch

- The orientation is very much based on a project management perspective, which is fine if you are one, but others may prefer to cherry-pick the most applicable ideas.
- Anyone who flies by the seat of their pants would have to be very disciplined to apply these ideas. It's a bit like dieting.

BOOK: *Sun Tzu; The Art Of War For Executives*
AUTHOR: Donald Krause

What the book says

- The ancient wisdom of this 2500-year-old text is invaluable commentary on such topics as leadership, strategy, organization, competition and cooperation.
- The ten principles for competitive success are:
  1. *Learn to fight* (against the competition).
  2. *Show the way* (leadership determines success).
  3. *Do it right* (all competitive advantage is based on effective execution).
  4. *Know the facts* (to achieve success, you must manage information).
  5. *Expect the worst* (do not assume the competition will not attack).
  6. *Seize the day* (the most important success factor is speed).
  7. *Burn the bridges* (position yourself where there is a danger of failing).
  8. *Do it better* (combine expected and unexpected tactics).
  9. *Pull together* (organization, training and communication are the foundations of success).
  10. *Keep them guessing* (the best competitive strategies have no form).

What's good about it

- It is interesting to apply the teachings of an ancient war expert to business, and in a modern context.

- The interpretations are clear and easily transferable to business matters.
- There are clear sections on planning, competitive strategy, conflict, control, positioning, flexibility and reputation.
- The overall message is: "Do not engage the enemy unless it is absolutely necessary." In other words, this is as much a book about the avoidance of war.

What you have to watch

- If taken the wrong way, the whole business of comparing war with business could lead to overly macho approaches. This is not really what the book is all about.
- There is a lot on using spies for information – this is clearly illegal.
- The book is obsessed with the competition ("the enemy"), whereas many would argue that it is more profitable to concentrate on what *you* are going to do, not the opposition.

BOOK: *The Art Of Creative Thinking*
AUTHOR: John Adair

What the book says

- Once you understand the creative process, you can train yourself to listen, look and read with a creative attitude. Techniques include:
  - Using the stepping stones of analogy (use normal things to suggest new uses).
  - Make the strange familiar and the familiar strange (analyse what you don't know about something you know well).
  - Widen your span of relevance (many inventions were conceived by those working in other fields).
  - Be constantly curious.
  - Practice serendipity (the more you think, the more it appears you are in "the right place at the right time").
  - Making better use of your *Depth Mind* (trust your subconscious to sort things out and generate solutions once you have "briefed it").
  - Learn to tolerate ambiguity.
  - Suspend judgement.
  - No one should wait for inspiration – you have to make it happen.

What's good about it

- This rather brilliant short book was originally written in 1990, so it is not riddled with modern jargon or method. It just tells it straight.

- Chance favours the prepared mind. By keeping your eyes open, listening for ideas and keeping a notebook, you can capture stimuli as they occur.
- It is full of inspirational comments from artists, scientists and philosophers:
    - *"I invent nothing; I rediscover."* Rodin
    - *"Everything has been thought of before, but the problem is to think of it again."* Goethe
    - *"Discovery consists of seeing what everyone has seen and thinking what nobody has thought."* Anon

What you have to watch

- Nothing. Everyone should read it for life use as well as just creative thinking in business.

BOOK: *The E Myth Revisited*
AUTHOR: **Michael Gerber**

What the book says

- Most small businesses don't work, and here's what to do about it.
- There are two big myths about people who start their own businesses:
  1. Most are entrepreneurs (they probably aren't).
  2. An individual who understands the technical work of a business can successfully run a business that does that technical work (this assumption is usually wrong and can be fatal).
- The Fatal Assumption:*if you understand the technical work of a business, you understand a business that does that technical work.*
- In fact, those running businesses need to be part entrepreneur, part manager, part technician. If they can't, then they need others to perform these roles. The first thinks ahead and dreams, the second controls and restrains, the third gets the work done.
- Businesses move from infancy (the technician's phase), to adolescence (getting some help), beyond the comfort zone to maturity.

What's good about it

- The turn-key revolution is a way of looking at your business that makes you behave like McDonalds from the very start. You have to record every little element that makes your business different and turn these into a virtue that is worth paying for.

- "Contrary to popular belief, my experience has shown me that the people who are exceptionally good in business aren't so because of what they know but because of their *insatiable need to know more.*"
- The idea of an *Entrepreneurial Seizure* is a good one. One day you suddenly ask *why am I doing this?* and start imagining your own business.
- The dilemma for many small business owners is that they don't own a business, they own a job, which essentially has no value.
- "The difference between creativity and innovation is the difference between thinking about getting things done in the world and getting things done."

What you have to watch

- This is all about small businesses, not the generalities of big business.

BOOK: *The Halo Effect*
AUTHOR: Phil Rosenzweig

What the book says

- Much of our business thinking is shaped by delusions – errors of logic and flawed judgements that distort our understanding of the real reasons behind a company's performance.
- These delusions affect the business press and academic research, as well as many bestselling books that promise to reveal the secrets of success or the path to greatness.
- The most pervasive delusion is the Halo Effect. When a company's sales and profits are up, people often conclude that it has a brilliant strategy, a visionary leader, capable employees and a superb corporate culture.
- When performance falters, they deduce the opposite but actually little may have changed. Other delusions are as follows.
- **Correlation and causality:** two things may be correlated but we may not know which causes which, or whether they are linked at all.
- **Single explanations:** there are usually many reasons for something, not just one.
- **Connecting the winning dots:** finding similar features in successful companies doesn't help because they can't be compared accurately with unsuccessful ones.
- **Rigorous research:** if the data aren't good, it doesn't matter how much analysis is done – the conclusions will still be false.
- **Lasting success:** is almost impossible to achieve – almost all high-performing companies regress over time, regardless of what they do.
- **Absolute performance:** performance is relative, not absolute. A company can improve and fall behind its rivals at the same time.

- **Wrong end of the stick:** successful companies may have highly focused strategies, but that doesn't mean such strategies guarantee success.
- **Organizational physics:** performance doesn't obey immutable laws of nature and cannot be predicted with the accuracy of science.

What's good about it

- This is a hugely thought-provoking book that questions many pieces of received wisdom.
- The analysis of *In Search of Excellence* and *Built To Last* may force you to review your opinion of these two famous business books.

What you have to watch

- Nothing. It's really worth reading.

BOOK: *The Laws Of Simplicity*
AUTHOR: John Maeda

What the book says

- Simplicity = Sanity. There are ten laws of simplicity:
  1. *Reduce.* The simplest way to achieve simplicity is through thoughtful reduction.
  2. *Organize.* Organization makes a system of many appear fewer.
  3. *Time.* Savings in time feel like simplicity.
  4. *Learn.* Knowledge makes everything simpler.
  5. *Differences.* Simplicity and complexity need each other.
  6. *Context.* What lies in the periphery of simplicity is definitely not peripheral.
  7. *Emotion.* More emotions are better than less.
  8. *Trust.* In simplicity we trust.
  9. *Failure.* Some things can never be made simple.
  10. *The One.* Simplicity is about subtracting the obvious, and adding the meaningful.

What's good about it

- The book is short, which it should be. It has a number of systems for reducing the complex down to simpler thinking. There are three keys:
  1. *Away.* More appears like less by simply moving it far away.
  2. *Open.* Openness simplifies complexity.
  3. *Power.* Use less, gain more.

- There are plenty of thought-provoking ideas to sort out complex things:
  - *How simple can you make it? vs. How complex does it have to be?*
  - *How can you make the wait shorter? vs. How can you make the wait more tolerable?*
  - SHE: Shrink, Hide, Embody.
  - SLIP: Sort, Label, Integrate, Prioritize.
  - BRAIN: Basics, Repeat, Avoid (desperation), Inspire, Never (forget to repeat).

What you have to watch

- The author has a preoccupation with technology, so many of the examples are technology-related.

BOOK: *The Pirate Inside*
AUTHOR: Adam Morgan

What the book says

- Powerful brands are built by people, not by proprietary methodologies.
- The real issue is not the strategy, but how we need to *behave* when an organization's systems seem more geared to slowing and diluting, than spurring and galvanizing.
- To achieve this you need to be a *Constructive Pirate*. This is not the same as anarchy where there are "no rules", but it requires a different set of rules.
- It shows how to write your own "Articles" in your organization.
- Even in big organizations, you need challenger subcultures.

What's good about it

- It explains nine ways of behaving that stimulate challenger brand cultures.
  1. **Outlooking** – looking for different kinds of insights by:

     Emotional Insertion. Putting a new kind of emotion into the category

     Overlay. Overlaying the rules of a different category onto your own

     Brand Neighbourhoods. Radically reframing your competitive set

Grip. Finding a place for the brand to gain traction in contemporary culture

2. **Pushing** – pushing ideas well beyond the norm.
3. **Projecting** – being consistent across far more media than the usual.
4. **Wrapping** – communicating less conventionally with customers.
5. **Denting** – respecting colleagues whilst making a real difference.
6. **Binding** – having a contract that ensures everyone comes with the idea.
7. **Leaning** – pushing harder for sustained commitment.
8. **Refusing** – having the passion to say no.
9. **Taking it personally** – a different professionalism that transcends corporate man.

- *Biting the Other Generals* is a good concept based on an anecdote from the Seven Years War. A brilliantly unconventional General, James Wolfe, proved himself one of the most talented military leaders King George III had. When some of Wolfe's detractors tried to undermine him by complaining that he was mad, the king replied: "Oh, he is mad, is he? Then I would he would bite some other of my generals."

- *The Three Buckets* is a good exercise whereby clients have to categorize all their existing projects into *Brilliant Basics*, *Compelling Differences* and *Changing the Game* – usually with poignant results.

What you have to watch

- Not much. This is an excellent book and you can use the exercises with pretty much any business.

BOOK: *The Seven-Day Weekend*
AUTHORS: Ricardo Semler

What the book says

- The author runs a massive set of companies in Brazil, and insists on working in an unconventional way.
- He likes to question everything:
  - Why are we able to answer emails on Sundays, but unable to go to the movies on Monday afternoons?
  - Why do we think the opposite of work is leisure, when in fact it is idleness?
  - Why doesn't money buy success if almost everyone measures their success in cash?
  - Why does our customized and carefully crafted credo look like everyone else's?
  - Why do we think intuition is so valuable and unique – and find no place for it as an official business instrument?

What's good about it

- There are some neat little tricks that you can implement straight away, such as always asking why three times in a row.
- It gives you an authoritative source on which to base radical ideas so that you can challenge staid working practices or conservative thinking.
- There are lots of ideas for maintaining staff loyalty and interest, such as:
  - *Retire a little* (take Friday afternoons off and offset it against retirement age).
  - *Up 'n Down Pay* (vary hours and pay to suit circumstances).

- *Work 'n Stop* (take long periods off but declare intention to return).
- Board meetings that always have two vacancies for any members of staff who want to attend.
- One piece of reverse psychology suggests that when anything untoward happens you should do nothing on the assumption that good sense will eventually sort it out.
- There are some catchy phrases such as "Corporate yo-yo dieting", the boom and bust cycles that companies always get themselves into.

What you have to watch

- He has only run his own company so he can only speak from that experience.
- He is probably a pain to work with, so not all his ideas could necessarily be implemented without causing havoc in most companies.

BOOK: *Why Entrepreneurs Should Eat Bananas*
AUTHOR: Simon Tupman

What the book says

- It has 101 inspirational ideas for growing your business and yourself.
- Take positive control of your life – don't let circumstances rule you.
- The three Ps: Professional skills, Purpose, Passion. You need to be able to tick all three to claim that you are happy in life and work. If not, make changes.
- Enthusiasm comes for the Greek en theos ("inner God").
- *"Nothing great was ever achieved without enthusiasm."* Ralph Waldo Emerson
- There are three types of people: those who make things happen, those who watch things happen, and those who wonder what happened.
- You need to see the world for what it is, examine best practice, connect with existing customers, find new ones, connect with your people if you have them, and then connect with life itself.

What's good about it

- You can dip into a point anywhere. Some of the best tips are:
  - Develop a "spoken logo" – this is your elevator pitch that goes beyond the factual and into the emotional benefit of what you do.
  - Burn your brochures – most of them serve no purpose and say the same thing.

- Start leading or consider leaving – negative people need to move on.
- Ask existing customers for referrals – many people never bother.
- Leave the office no later than 5.30 – it's amazing what you can do if you do.
- Understand your value – too many people undervalue themselves.
- Keep on moving – a health point: the more you move, the healthier you are.
- There are lots of different forms in the appendix that you can use, such as customer surveys, self-assessments and team performance questionnaires.

What you have to watch

- The title is a misnomer. The only reason for the title is to catch your attention and the answer is simply that bananas are good for you, which is a bit of a let down.
- It's not really about entrepreneurs – it is to do with anyone who works in a company.

Index